SHAKESPEARE AND THE BOOK

Shakespeare and the Book is a lively and learned account of Shakespeare's plays as they were transformed from scripts to be performed into books to be read, and eventually from popular entertainments into the centerpieces of the English literary canon. Kastan examines the material forms in which we encounter Shakespeare, exploring with unusual breadth and elegance the motives and activities of Shakespeare's first publishers, the curious eighteenth-century schizophrenia that saw Shakespeare performed almost always in versions adapted for contemporary tastes even as scholars were working to establish and restore the "genuine" texts of the plays, and also the exhilarating possibilities of electronic media for presenting Shakespeare to new generations of readers.

This is an important contribution to Shakespearean textual scholarship, to the history of the early English book trade, and to the theory of drama itself. As it considers the various forms in which Shakespeare is available to be read, *Shakespeare and the Book* persuades its readers of the resiliency of the book itself as a technology and of Shakespeare's own extraordinary resiliency, which has been made possible not least by print.

DAVID SCOTT KASTAN is Professor of English and Comparative Literature at Columbia University. He is a specialist on Shakespeare and early modern culture. His most recent book is *Shakespeare After Theory* (1999) and his other publications include *Shakespeare and the Shapes of Time* (1981), *Staging the Renaissance* (1991, edited with Peter Stallybrass), *Critical Essays on Shakespeare's "Hamlet"* (1995), *The New History of Early English Drama* (1997, edited with John Cox, and winner of the 1998 ATHE award for the best book on theatre history), and *A Companion to Shakespeare* (1999).

SHAKESPEARE AND THE BOOK

DAVID SCOTT KASTAN

Columbia University

PUBLISHED BY THE PRESS SYNDICATE OF THE UNIVERSITY OF CAMBRIDGE
The Pitt Building, Trumpington Street, Cambridge, United Kingdom

CAMBRIDGE UNIVERSITY PRESS
The Edinburgh Building, Cambridge CB2 2RU, UK
40 West 20th Street, New York, NY 10011–4211, USA
10 Stamford Road, Oakleigh, VIC 3166, Australia
Ruiz de Alarcón 13, 28014 Madrid, Spain
Dock House, The Waterfront, Cape Town 8001, South Africa

http://www.cambridge.org

First published 2001

Printed in the United Kingdom at the University Press, Cambridge

Typeface Monotype Baskerville 11/12.5 pt.   *System* QuarkXPress™   [SE]

A catalogue record for this book is available from the British Library

ISBN 0 521 78139 6 hardback
ISBN 0 521 78651 7 paperback

For Stephen Orgel and Keith Walker

Contents

List of illustrations   *page* viii
Acknowledgements   xi

Introduction   1

1   From playhouse to printing house; or, making a good
    impression   14

2   From quarto to folio; or, size matters   50

3   From contemporary to classic; or, textual healing   79

4   From codex to computer; or, presence of mind   111

Notes   137
Index   159

Illustrations

1. Sir Anthony Van Dyck, "Sir John Suckling." 1632/1641, oil on canvas, 216.5 × 130.2 cm. Copyright The Frick Collection, New York and used with permission. *page* 12

2. Ben Jonson, *Every Man Out of his Humor* (1600), title page, STC 14767; used through the courtesy of The Huntington Library and Art Gallery. 18

3. *Henry V* (1600), title page, STC 22289; used through the courtesy of The Huntington Library and Art Gallery. 19

4. Q2 *Hamlet* (1604), title page, STC 22276; used through the courtesy of The Folger Shakespeare Library. 28

5. *Love's Labor's Lost* (1598), title page, STC 22294; used through the courtesy of The Folger Shakespeare Library. 32

6. *King Lear* (1608), title page, STC 22292; used through the courtesy of The Folger Shakespeare Library. 34

7. *King Leir* (1605), title page, STC 5343; used through the courtesy of The Folger Shakespeare Library. 36

8. *The London Prodigal* (1605), title page, STC 22333; used through the courtesy of Trinity College, Cambridge. 37

9. *The Troublesome Reign of King John* (1591), title page, STC 14644; used through the courtesy of Trinity College, Cambridge. 38

10. *The Troublesome Reign of King John* (1622), title page, STC 14647; used through the courtesy of Trinity College, Cambridge. 39

11. *Romeo and Juliet* (1599), title page, STC 22323; used through the courtesy of The Folger Shakespeare Library. 41

12. *Romeo and Juliet*, (1622?), Q4 title page, STC 22325; used through the courtesy of The Huntington Library and Art Gallery. 42

13. *Romeo and Juliet* (1622?), Q4 variant title page, STC 22325a; used through the courtesy of The Huntington Library and Art Gallery. 43

14. *The Passionate Pilgrim* (1612), title page, STC 22343; used through the courtesy of The Folger Shakespeare Library. 57

15. *The Passionate Pilgrim* (1612), title page cancel, STC 22343; used through the courtesy of the Bodleian Library, Oxford University. 58

16. *Henry V* 1619 Pavier quarto title page (falsely dated 1608), used through the courtesy of Columbia University. 59

17. 1623 Shakespeare folio title page, STC 22273; used through the courtesy of Columbia University. 70

18. Nahum Tate, *King Lear* (1681), sig. E3ᵛ; used through the courtesy of The Folger Shakespeare Library. 87

19. Lewis Theobald, *Double Falsehood* (1728), title page; used through the courtesy of The Folger Shakespeare Library. 94

20. William Warburton (ed.), *The Works of Shakespear* (1747), title page; used through the courtesy of Columbia University. 104

21. *1 Henry IV*, in *The Works of Shakespeare*, ed. Nicholas Rowe (1709) vol. 3, p. 1177; used through the courtesy of Columbia University. 105

22. "First Variorum," *Plays and Poems of William Shakespeare* (London, 1803), vol. 11, pp. 362–3; used through the courtesy of Columbia University. 106

23. Advertisement for *The Plays of William Shakespeare*, ed. Samuel Johnson and George Steevens; opposite title page, George Steevens (ed.), *Six Old Source Plays of Shakespeare* (London, 1779); used through the courtesy of The Folger Shakespeare Library. 108

24. Hypertext page, "*King Lear*" (Columbia University, Literature/Humanities); used through the courtesy of Richard Sacks. 126

Acknowledgements

This book began as the Lord Northcliffe Lectures that I was privileged to deliver at University College, London in March 1999. My delight at having been invited to give the lectures can hardly be overestimated. (I wish I could confidently attribute the same delight to those who heard them, but they will have to, if asked, speak for themselves.) I am grateful to all at UCL who made that occasion so memorable, but especially to Professors David Trotter and John Sutherland, who in fact were responsible not only for my invitation but also for the extraordinary hospitality I was shown on my visit.

Their responsibility goes deeper, however, than for merely arranging what was a wonderful experience for me, as their own work, in different ways, provided much of the inspiration for my consideration of Shakespeare and the book. Though both are usually more concerned with nineteenth- and twentieth-century literature than with anything directly related to my topic here, they both have long been thinking about literature's materiality in ways that provoked my interest in what became this study. John Sutherland, the current Lord Northcliffe Professor, has provocatively pointed to and worked to fill what he sometime ago identified as a "large and troubling hole" at the center of literary sociology: "scholarly ignorance about book trade and publishing history technicalities." The chapters here record my debt to that observation and my desire to remedy at least my own ignorance of the topic. David Trotter's work is perhaps less obviously connected to my own, but his work, not least his recent study of "mess," has always combined an extraordinary sensitivity both to the words on the page and to the intellectual and institutional conditions necessary for them to appear there. And "mess" is a topic any scholar can all too easily identify with, or at least can any scholar's family or friends who have unsuspectingly ventured into the study as a book is being written.

Others who must be acknowledged perhaps bear less immediate responsibility for what appears here, although they were no less influential, as they were the friends whom I talked with, listened to, read, and no doubt often bothered as my own interests in Shakespeare and the book were developing: David Bevington, Peter Blayney, Margreta de Grazia, Andrew Murphy, Franco Moretti, Barbara Mowat, Richard Proudfoot, Peter Stallybrass, G. Thomas Tanselle, Paul Werstine, Henry Woudhuysen, and Steve Zwicker; and, perhaps most significantly, a group of extraordinary young scholars who, as they passed through Columbia's halls and after, have played instructor to my eager student at least as often as it was the other way round: Heidi Brayman Hackel, Douglas Brooks, Patricia Cahill, Alan Farmer, András Kiséry, Jesse Lander, Zachary Lesser, Ben Robinson, Andrew Sage, Bill Sherman (who still counts as young), and Chloe Wheatley. All of these people will find in the pages that follow places where they will disagree with my ideas and my formulations, and, no doubt, find others where "my ideas and my formulations" are in fact theirs. In regard to the former, I can only utter the formulaic assurance that they must not be held responsible for the limitations of the book; in regard to the latter, I suppose could merely take the disclaimer back, but in fairness I must say thanks.

There are other friends who have importantly contributed, friends who often did no more, but always no less, than to believe in me and in the project, and without whom this book might never have been written (or, more likely, without whom it might have been written more quickly but with far less pleasure and confidence): David Armitage, Kimberley Coles, Josie Dixon, Jessica Hodge, Jonathan Hope, Gordon McMullan, Claire McEachern, and Jim Shapiro so prominent among these that their welcomed distractions must be publicly recognized.

I am also more grateful than I can say for the courtesy, generosity, flexibility, good-humor, and stunning knowledge of the staffs at the various libraries in which I have done most of the work on this book: Columbia University's Rare Book Room, the Folger

Shakespeare Library, the Huntington Library and Art Gallery, and the British Library. Some of their assistance is recognized in the picture credits, but that represents only a very small piece of their actual contribution, among which not the least is their creation of environments in which one can believe that scholarship still matters (and in which it can be efficiently done: the remarkable collections in all those places enabled me not only to consult the editions that are the main subject of this study, many of which are extremely rare, some unique, but also enabled me to engage with the generations of critics who have worked on similar problems, to whom my debts can only partially be acknowledged in my notes).

And there is my family who must be thanked, who good-naturedly – I think – tolerated long periods of me being away at various libraries or in front of the computer (and in my absences and intensities walked the dog); and the two people to whom this book is dedicated, whose extraordinary generosity in different ways made it possible.

One last note: I have considerably revised the texts of what I gave as the Lord Northcliffe lectures, as well as the paper I presented at the International Shakespeare Congress in August 2000, which served as an early version of chapter three. My hope is that whatever has been achieved in revision towards greater clarity and precision will outweigh whatever has been lost in abandoning the more informal nature of the original lectures (some of whose marks I could not quite bear to part with). Again, I give sincere thanks not only to those who organized those opportunities for me to speak, but also to the audiences on each occasion, whose alert, learned, and sometimes very unnerving questions and comments, have also served to make this work far better than it ever would have been without them.

Introduction

Shakespeare and the Book is a seemingly straightforward title, exceptional, perhaps, only in its conspicuous avoidance of the usual allusiveness of academic title-making. The words are all simple (the very familiar proper name alone having more than one syllable) and its structure is certainly conventional enough: two nouns joined by a copulative. The title ought to reveal clearly what the book is about, but I am not sure it does. Or, rather, I am sure it does, but I also fear that many readers won't realize it right away. The "and" is the problem.

To start with the second term: by itself, "the book" hardly needs justification as an object of interest. It is a hot topic in the academy today, even in the popular press. It should always have been so, because the book is one of the major achievements of our humanity. For too long, however, its consideration has been shunted off to unpopular bibliography courses or hidden among the offerings of the library school. But suddenly the book has become important to us all, if only because the insistent claims of its imminent demise have focused our attention upon what we will lose with its passing.

While the book's monopoly over the written word was unchallenged, its ubiquitous presence seemed natural and inevitable; but the book itself was largely invisible. Belatedly we have come to see it in its own right – as an artifact, as a commodity, and as a technology. Its new-found visibility registers in the widely circulated e-jokes: the book wittily reimagined in techno-speak. "Bio-Optic Organized Knowledge (trade name: BOOK)" is hailed as a remarkable technological breakthrough: a "revolutionary information platform" requiring neither wires nor batteries; it is portable and compact yet "powerful enough to hold as much information as a CD-ROM disk"; its "opaque paper technology" allows a "doubling of information density"; each page is "scanned optically." You get the idea.

Ironically (or is it inevitably?), not only the book's advantages but also its history have become compelling objects of interest at the precise moment when we are being confidently assured that its demise is near. Printed books, we are told, no less than libraries and bookshops, are dinosaurs that do not yet know they are extinct. William J. Mitchell, Dean at the Architectural School at MIT, for example, sees a world in which books themselves have no cultural value but are mere pacifiers, as he says wryly, for those "addicted to the look and feel of tree flakes encased in dead cow."[1] Many voices have joined in to sing the book's eclipse, as print moves forever "beyond Gutenberg"; nonetheless, it is unmistakably a song in counterpoint: an enthusiastic soprano line for the digiphiles, celebrating our epistemological and political release from the tyranny of the codex, and a despairing bass part reserved for the digi-phobes, proclaiming the inevitable loss of authority, coherence, and sensual delight as the written word is reduced to bits and bytes.

In chapter four I will have more to say about the transition from the institutions and technologies of print to their digital substitutes, thinking about what may be lost and gained as words appear to us not conformed as ink on paper but as pixels on computer screens. But for now I will say only that, in spite of the exhilarating potential of the electronic text and the seeming irresistibility of its technologies, the book's resiliency may have been seriously underestimated. We are perhaps living in the latter days of print, but the now seemingly antiquated technology of the book may very well prove more robust than many have imagined. In any case, if we are to offer compelling alternatives to it, we must understand how it functions in its full material and social complexity. In part these chapters are designed to contribute to that understanding.

They begin with what is, or should be, a self-evident assertion: that the material form and location in which we encounter the written word are active contributors to the meaning of what is read. A poem read as it was written by its author in ink on a sheet of foolscap is not identical with the "same" poem read as printed in the Complete Works of the poet, or as published in the Norton anthology, or even as it is read online. Not only is it likely that the so-called accidentals of the texts will vary (if not some things more obviously substantive), but also that the modes and matrices of presentation themselves inevitably become part of the poem's structures of meaning, part, that is, of what determines how it is understood and valued. In D. F. McKenzie words, "its presentation in different formats and typefaces, on different papers in different bindings, and its sale at different times, places, and prices, imply distinct conditions and uses and must vary the meanings its readers make of it."[2] This probably should be obvious, but in literary studies there has long been a tendency to act as if the works we read have a reality independent of the physical texts in which we engage them. In an essay that served as a cornerstone of the New Criticism, René Wellek and Austin Warren off-handedly dismissed as a "theory which probably has not many serious adherents today" the idea that the literary work existed as "the writing on the paper" or "on the printed page."[3]

Their "today" is not our today, of course, but still it is usual, at least in the classroom-teaching of literature, to ignore the material contexts in which it is presented to its readers, to assume (or merely tactically to pretend) that it exists exclusively as the patterning of its language apart from its particular appearance "on the paper" or its location on a particular "printed page" (or on a computer screen, or even as it is spoken). If physical texts even rate a mention, they are usually considered to be at best conveyors of the work and at worst corruptors of it. Nonetheless, the specific forms and contexts in which we encounter literature, its modes and mechanisms of transmission, are intrinsic aspects of what it is, not considerations wholly external to it; and, no less than its semantic and syntactic organization, these exert influence over our judgments and interpretations. Yet even editorial theory, which of all areas of literary studies might be thought the most sensitive to the inescapability of the material text, easily posits as its object of desire a work that never was, an ideal text of an author's intentions that no materialization does (or can) bear witness to.

I am deeply suspicious of this commitment, however much the logic of its defenders may appeal. No actual text can, of course,

perfectly articulate the intentions of the author, and its defects are
at least theoretically liable to correction; but the concomitant argument that the author's unrealized intentions are therefore the work
itself – and their materialization merely some approximation of
the intended work, at best instructions for imagining the intangible
original – seems to me to be true only tautologically.[4] It is true, that
is, only if the work is defined as the fully articulate intentions of the
author whether or not these are embodied in any particular text.
Such a definition of the "work" is not logically impossible, and
indeed it is not without value; but it does serve to isolate the work
of art from most of the actual conditions of its making, granting
its author an almost impossible sovereignty over it. The work is
denied any effective principle of realization, seemingly imagined
as something self-sufficient, and, in the process, the contexts in
which it was written and in which it is read are, perhaps unwit-
tingly, universalized.

   I would argue, on the contrary, that literature exists, in any useful
sense, only and always in its materializations, and that these are the
conditions of its meaning rather than merely the containers of it.
Though the imagination may desire something less coarse than the
various physical texts that no doubt inadequately preserve and
present its workings (like Wordsworth's "mind" seeking "Some
element to stamp her image on / In nature somewhat nearer to her
own"[5]), it must content itself with a medium that is incommensu-
rate with its refinement. Only as texts are realized materially are
they accessible. Only then can they delight and mean. The work of
the imagination is unable to constitute itself; it is always dependent
upon imperfect physical supports for it to be presented to its
readers, supports that themselves mediate what is there to be
engaged.

   Some might say that this focus on the physical forms in which
literature circulates and on the conditions that govern both its production and consumption is a sociological rather than a properly
literary concern, deflecting attention away from the internal design
of the text to the circumstantial details of its manufacture. But of
course "the text" is exactly what is at issue. It is, I hope, not too
stubbornly literal to insist that the literary text must be read as a
physical object and therefore cannot be, except theoretically, seg-

regated from the circumstantial details that bring it to our attention. We can read only what is physically before our eyes to be read, and we should, therefore, factor into our calculus of meaning what Roger Chartier calls "the effects that material forms produce."[6]

Attention to how the material forms in which the text circulates affect meaning does not in any way deny the importance of its symbolic patterning, somehow refusing its "literariness" in favor of its social existence; rather, precisely what such attention seeks is a more comprehensive conception than is otherwise possible of its literariness, of the palpable designs it has upon its readers. Such attention should expand, not in any way limit, our understanding of the text. It recognizes that the specific forms of a text's embodiment – things as vulgarly material as typeface, format, layout, design, even paper (think of William Prynne's outrage that editions of Shakespeare were printed on "farre better paper than most Octavo or Quarto Bibles"[7]) – are not external to the meaning of the text, inert vehicles designed only for its conveyance, but rather are part of the text's structures of signification.

Focus on the documentary particularities of a text frees our reading from the fantasy of literary autonomy. It demystifies the act of writing, clarifying the actual conditions of creativity, locating the text within a network of intentions, within which the author's, however dominant, are still only some among many – and intentions, it should be noted, that are incapable of producing the book itself. The specific forms of textual embodiment speak the complex history of its making, and speak as well the remarkable productivity of the medium, a useful reminder of how much the book, no less than any of the electronic media that threaten to replace it, is a technology that not merely passively conveys its content but one that actively shapes its very intelligibility.

But if at this time attention to "the book" can hardly be surprising, indeed is almost obligatory as its protracted dominance over the written word is now perceived to be under threat, the application of my interest in the printed book to the primary term of my concern here – Shakespeare – arguably is. At least in his role as playwright, Shakespeare had no obvious interest in the printed book. Performance was the only form of publication he sought for his plays. He made no effort to have them published and none to stop the publication of the often poorly printed versions that did reach the bookstalls. In chapters one and two I will explore the motivations and activities of the people who, for their own reasons having almost nothing to do with Shakespeare's literary merits, first brought his plays into print. A lot of names, many unfamiliar to all but textual scholars, will appear on those pages, names of people who were responsible for the fact that we have Shakespeare to read at all, and whose motives and actions have fashioned what is there for us to read. Shakespeare himself seemingly did not care.

My interest in Shakespeare and the book, then, risks appearing as at best a quirky antiquarianism and at worse as a perverse self-indulgence (since by "the book" I mean precisely that – the physical text itself, as both artifact and commodity – rather than using it metaphorically to point to the plays, as many have, as complex verbal structures). Indeed, M. C. Bradbrook has stated explicitly that to treat the drama "as book-art is to do it great violence."[8] Clearly, Shakespeare's own commitment to print was reserved for his narrative poetry.[9] His *Venus and Adonis* and *Lucrece* were published in carefully printed editions by his fellow townsman, Richard Field, and to each volume Shakespeare contributed a signed dedication. The published plays, however, show no sign of Shakespeare's involvement. He wrote them for the theater and not for a reading public; they were scripts to be acted not plays to be read. "It is in performance that the plays lived and had their being," writes Stanley Wells. "Performance is the end to which they were created."[10] On such seemingly solid ground, many teachers and scholars have rested their confidence that the proper focus of academic attention should, therefore, be performance-based, either considering the printed play as what Michael Goldman calls "a design for performance" or considering performance itself as the object of study (in the theater or, more often, for obvious reasons, on video or film).[11]

There is much to be said for such a focus, and much – too much, I often think in my most curmudgeonly moments following long hours in the theater watching dutiful, or, often worse, all-too imaginative productions of Shakespeare – has been said for it. Shakespeare does, of course, "live" in the theater; there he becomes our contemporary, responsive to our needs and interests. But, as I have argued elsewhere, that seems to be exactly what makes the commitment to stage-centered approaches to Shakespeare suspect. Shakespeare in performance yields too easily to our desires. The fact of Shakespeare's domination of the theatrical repertory in Britain from the mid-eighteenth century to the present alone speaks the pliancy of his plays in the hands of theater professionals. In the theater Shakespeare escapes his historicity, becoming for every age a contemporary playwright, and arguably its most important one. Like the promiscuous Hero of Claudio's tortured imagination, he is not merely our Shakespeare, he is everybody's Shakespeare.[12]

Print is a more conservative medium. I mean that literally, not morally or politically; it *conserves* in a way performance can not. Whatever else print does, it provides a durable image of the text, one that avoids the necessary evanescence of performance; indeed its ability to conserve is, in large part, what has made continued performance possible. The text lasts on the page in a way it cannot in the theater, its endurance at once the sign and the foundation of its greater resistance to appropriation. The printed text remains before our eyes, demanding to be respected. This is not to say that the printed play is more authentic than the performed play, nor is it to say that it is somehow immune to tendentious interpretation. Editions and readings of them, as I will explore in chapter three, are no less affected by contemporary interests and understandings than are productions. It is merely to point to the obvious: that the printed text fixes in time and space the words that performance releases as the very condition of its being.

But there is, perhaps, something less obvious to say about the relationship of text and performance.[13] Although they have often been imagined as two halves of a single reality, as the inner and outer aspects of the play, the printed text and the performed play are not related as origin and effect (in whatever order one might conceive it). Indeed, in any precise sense, they do not constitute the same entity. Performance no more animates the text than does the text record the performance. They are dissimilar and discontinuous modes of production. Their incommensurability is uncannily registered on the title page of John Webster's *The Duchess of Malfi* (1623), where the play is said to be published *"As it was Presented priuately, at the Blackfriers; and publiquely at the Globe, By the* Kings Maiesties Seruants," and yet also said to be "The perfect and exact Coppy, with diuerse *things Printed, that the length of the Play* would not beare in the Presentment." The title page makes two different and incompatible claims about the text it prints: it is impossibly offered both "as it was Presented" and as it was *not* presented, that is, with more than the play "would . . . beare in the Presentment."

But that paradoxical double claim – the "Bifold authority" that Robert Weimann has taken from *Troilus and Cressida* 5.2.151 to name the text's competing structures of authorization (a phrase that appears in the folio as "By foule authority," the variant speaking the inevitable inadequacy of those structures) – exposes something of the perplexing riddle of the relation of print and performance.[14] Neither one is the effect of the other; neither reproduces, or draws upon (except rhetorically) the other's claim to authenticity. The printed play is neither a pre-theatrical text nor a post-theatrical one; it is a *non*-theatrical text, even when it claims to offer a version of the play "as it was played."

As it was played, it existed in the theater, in the ephemeral sounds and gestures of dramatic action. The printed text can never be the play "as it was played." It is always, necessarily if tautologically, the play as printed; and as printed it ties its readers to the words on the page. Its conventions do not arrest performance, while anticipating its eventual release on stage, but, rather, they defer or, even better, deny performance altogether. Reading a play is not reading performance (the printed play as textualized drama) or even reading *for* performance (the printed play as potential drama); it is reading in the absence of performance (the printed play as . . . well, the printed play). "If the play is a book," says Stephen Orgel decisively, "it's not a play."[15]

The performed play, conversely, can never be merely a realization of the play as printed. It is neither a pre-textual version of the play nor a post-textual one. Dr. Johnson famously claimed that "a dramatic exhibition is a book recited,"[16] but this is merely evidence of Johnson's characteristic textual, rather than theatrical, orientation. Even when "a dramatic exhibition" takes as its playing text a particular print manifestation, it does not merely vitalize that text. It does not apply the warming fire of production to dramatic possibilities somehow frozen on the page. Performance *makes* something that did not previously exist, rather than *enacts* something that has a prior reality; and what it makes, as Terry Eagleton says, "cannot be mechanically extrapolated from an inspection of the text itself."[17]

Text and performance are, then, not partial and congruent aspects of some unity that we think of as the play, but are two discrete modes of production. Performance operates according to a theatrical logic of its own rather than one derived from the text; the printed play operates according to a textual logic that is not derived from performance. In considering a performance of *Hamlet* and an edition of *Hamlet*, one is not, I think, considering two iterations of a single work. Though they are admittedly related (certainly more closely than are, say, a performance of *Hamlet* and an edition of *Othello*), they are still materially and theoretically distinct. *Hamlet* is not a pre-existent entity that the text and performance each *contain*, but the name that each calls what it brings into being. Neither is more or less authentic than the other, for there is no external reality, apart from the texts and the performances themselves, that can provide a standard against which that authenticity might be measured.

We cannot think, then, of the printed text as something secondary, or as something as yet unrealized, ceding authority to the performed play as the fulfillment of the text's mere potential, any more than we can assume the priority of the text, granting it, as Dr. Johnson would have us do, preeminence over performance. But we must concede that the text has its own compelling logic and history. Not only theoretically but also historically, the text of Shakespeare's plays can claim, not precedence over performance, but parity with it. Although Shakespeare did indeed write his plays to be performed, they quickly escaped his control, surfacing as books to be read and allowing Shakespeare to "live" no less vitally in print than he does in the theater. If the 1623 folio is a memorial tribute, "an office to the dead," as John Heminge and Henry Condell say in their dedicatory epistle (sig. A2ᵛ), it is one in which the departed is brought back to life by the very act of publication. "Thou art aliue still," says Jonson in his commendatory poem in the folio, "while thy Booke doth liue." In print, Shakespeare is not merely remembered but revived.

How powerfully the book has become Shakespeare's milieu may be judged by a quick look at two visual images. The first is a stained-glass window, a photograph of which serves as the cover of this book. The image is, in many ways, unsurprising. It is yet one more sign of Shakespeare's inescapability, one more institutional recognition of his centrality in our culture. And yet it is in many ways a strange representation. It is, of course, unmistakably Shakespeare; the features are familiar, the dress characteristic. The setting, however, is odd, or at least odd for Shakespeare; it is an indoor scene, with a marble pillar to Shakespeare's right and an open window through which one can see a tree. It is not, as one might have expected, obviously either a theatre or a study; it is neither a site of playing nor of writing. And Shakespeare's posture is odder still. Shakespeare faces forward, his legs crossed above his ankles. His right elbow rests on a stack of books, which themselves are sitting on a waist-high marble plinth. The index finger of Shakespeare's left hand points towards a manuscript scroll extending from beneath the stacked volumes. The books are the surprise, conspicuously interposed between Shakespeare and the handwritten scroll. We often see pictures of Shakespeare writing; his quill pen is as much part of his iconography as the keys are of St. Peter's. But Shakespeare is rarely associated visually with printed books. Manuscript was his medium, not print. He wrote his scripts longhand, and scribes produced additional handwritten copies of the plays as well as the scrolls containing individual actors' parts (though the blocks of writing on the scroll in the window seem to mark it as something other than a play script). Shakespeare was a theater professional, not a literary man.

This is what are told again and again. It is, however, only a half truth. The other half is that Shakespeare was, almost from the first, a best-selling dramatist. By the time of his death, over forty editions of his plays had reached print, and three – *Richard II, Richard III,* and *1 Henry IV* – had been published in five or more editions. If these numbers seem modest before the twenty-four editions of William Baldwin's *Treatise of Moral Philosophy* published by 1640 or the forty plus editions of Lewis Bayley's *The Practice of Piety*, they still mark Shakespeare as a remarkably successful author. If it was not a role he sought for himself, or even from which he benefited much, it was one he could not escape. His plays found their way into print because of (and indeed their texts were in various ways configured by) the activities of the English book trade. The window speaks to that often-overlooked other half – that Shakespeare's legitimate medium is not merely the theater but also, if not primarily, the book.

And well the handsome stained-glass window might choose that particular half of the story to tell, as it graces a wall in the guild-hall of the Stationers' Company. It seems only fair that the Stationers have thus honored Shakespeare: not only because he is arguably the greatest of English literary figures, but also because he is arguably the industry's greatest cash cow. Certainly no other English author has made publishers so much money and received so little in return. Shakespeare has become one of the world's most popular writers and managed never to collect a penny in royalties. In a sense, this book can be understood as a examination of what determines the eccentric imagery of the Stationers' window: the interests and activities that took Shakespeare's plays out of the theater and brought them into the study, preserving and present-ing them to be read.

There is a second picture that might help explain what this book is about and help justify the conjunction of the two nouns of its title: a full-length portrait of Sir John Suckling by Anthony Van Dyck, painted about 1638 and hanging now in The Frick Museum in New York City (see Fig. 1). It is a wonderful painting, lusciously rendered. In 1661, John Aubrey described it as "a piece of great value," a portrait of Suckling "all at length, leaning against a rock, with a play-book, contemplating."[18] Suckling stands, gazing to his right, in an outcropping of large boulders. He is dressed in a blue silk tunic, with a red cloak around his shoulders; and he rests a large book on a rock. His left hand is at the book's upper-left corner, holding down about half its pages; his right holds up the bottom of a single leaf, revealing the double-columned page beneath that sits atop the remainder of the thick folio volume. The running title of the right-hand page exposed by the lifted leaf is marked "HAMLET," and a label protrudes from the volume's fore-edge with a word written in Roman majuscules: "SHAKSPERE." The name functions in a complicated way here. It may well be the first

1. Sir Anthony Van Dyck, "Sir John Suckling." 1632/1641, oil on canvas, 216.5 × 130.2 cm. Copyright The Frick Collection, New York and used with permission.

secular book that is explicitly identified in a painting, but in any case it clearly reveals Shakespeare's capacity to lend cultural prestige only some twenty-odd years after his death.[19] But it reveals no less clearly that the prestige he offers is already less a function of memorable plays enjoyed in the theater by millions (even by 1638) than of their existence in print. "SHAKSPERE" in Van Dyck's portrait names not a man but a book, and it is the complex cultural process that made this metonymy possible, as well as some of its implications and effects, that *Shakespeare and the Book* explores.

CHAPTER ONE

From playhouse to printing house; or, making a good impression

– Who's that?
– No one. The author.
Shakespeare in Love

The joke from the popular film is obvious enough, though it always gets a laugh. The film's invented investor, Fennyman, asks about a person that he has noticed standing on stage, and Henslowe replies that he is "No one," just "the author." What is funny, of course, is not merely that Henslowe thinks of the author as "no one," but that the particular "no one" that Fennyman has pointed to is Shakespeare, who more than any person of that era, has become unmistakably *someone* – and someone precisely because he has pre-eminently become The Author. Shakespeare was, not surprisingly, "the man of the millennium" in many polls as the zeros of the year 2000 rolled into view. The familiar image of a man with a receding hairline and shiny forehead, a ruff around his neck, and a quill pen in hand serves not only to identify Shakespeare "the author" but increasingly has become an emblem of human creativity itself.

But the film's joke also speaks an often overlooked truth. Within the collaborative economies of the early modern theatre, an author – even Shakespeare – was, if not exactly "no one," hardly the cynosure of the cultural world, hardly even "the author," as we have come to know that role, of his plays. It was an actors' theatre: Richard Burbage and Edward Alleyn were the celebrities of the age, rather than Shakespeare and Marlowe. Playwrighting was a kind of piece-work, providing the scripts for an emerging entertainment industry, scripts that legally belonged to the theatre companies and which were inevitably subjected to the contingencies of performance. Even Shakespeare, a sharer in the company for which he wrote during most of his career, would have had his plays altered as they remained in the repertory – cut, revised, modified for specific playing locations and occasions – alterations that may or may not have originated with him or have even received his approval. Certainly as the plays stayed in the repertory after his retirement from the company around 1612 and death in 1616, hands other than his own determined what was played.

Shakespeare's lack of interest in publishing his plays is tacit acknowledgement of the performative aspect of drama, if not also of the inescapable collaborations of its realization. Perhaps reluctant to claim an authority over them that he did not have by seeing them into print, Shakespeare contented himself with their availability in the theatre. Their plasticity there may well have seemed to him truer to their nature than the fixity they would achieve on the printed page.[1]

Certainly in the theatre, in the various forms in which they have been played, they have had a long and successful run. But if Shakespeare cared little about their publication, it should not be forgotten that their theatrical longevity has been in part enabled because the plays did reach print. Although arguably Shakespeare does not "live" on the page quite as vitally as he does in the theater, at very least we must grant that in print he is *preserved*. It is not an entirely happy metaphor, I admit. Living beings are preferable to mummies, and print, in any case, does not preserve language as firmly as formaldehyde preserves bodies. Nonetheless, without print there is no Shakespeare for all time. It is in the printing house that his scattered "limbs" are collected and cured, as Heminge and Condell say, re-membered as a body of work.

Such re-membering is of course no more exact than any other act of memory. Psychologists know that memory is never a perfect witness to the event remembered; it represses, displaces, and falsifies; nonetheless it is informative, though less as an objective representation of the event than as the overdetermined register of the event's reception and assimilation. Print remembers similarly; it too falsifies even as it recalls and records, incorporating elements separate from that which it would overtly remember. The Shakespeare remembered in the printing house is inevitably something other than Shakespeare – both more and less than his

originary presence. His corpus is reconstructed by sets of motivations and practices that leave their marks upon the text, distorting
it even as they preserve and set it forth.

This is not to return to the notion of an ideal text independent
of the processes of its materialization; it is to recognize that the
text, like the past, is never available in unmediated form. This
mediation is precisely what marks it as text, exactly as that which
marks the past as past is the impossibility of an unmediated
engagement with it. We, of course, engage Shakespeare only in
mediated form. One could say that this means that we never actually engage Shakespeare, but to the degree that this is true it is
merely an uninteresting literalism. Shakespeare is available precisely because "Shakespeare," in any meaningful sense other than
the biographical, is – and has always been – a synecdoche for the
involved mediations of the playhouse and printing house through
which he is produced.

The printed plays that preserve Shakespeare for us are all in
various ways deficient, yet, precisely in their distance from the ideal
text of editorial desire (and, as that desire projects it, authorial
intention), they witness to the complex conditions of authorship
that shaped his theatrical career. Shakespeare has become virtually
the iconic name for authorship itself, but he wrote in circumstances
in which his individual achievement was inevitably dispersed into
– if not compromised by – the collaborations necessary for both
play and book production. Nonetheless, Shakespeare's apparent
indifference to the publication of his plays, his manifest lack of
interest in reasserting his authority over them, suggests how little
he had invested in the notions of individuated authorship that,
ironically, his name has come so triumphantly to represent.
Literally his investment was elsewhere: in the lucrative partnership
of the acting company. He worked comfortably within its necessary collaborations, and clearly felt no need to claim his play texts
as his own as they began to circulate in print and be read.

In this regard, Shakespeare is perhaps somewhat more anoma-
lous than many have supposed. While no doubt the great majority
of playwrights "had no mind to be a man in Print," as Robert
Davenport says of himself in his preface "To the knowing Reader"
of *King John and Matilda* (1655), many playwrights did not merely

allow but actively sought publication to restore their intentions to the play they had written. Although all playwrights would have anticipated that their plays would be shaped by the demands of performance, their scripts legally being the property of the acting company (and the genre itself, as we are often reminded, existing as a subliterary form perhaps incapable of sustaining the burden of literary ambition), many playwrights consciously turned to print to preserve their creation in its intended form.

Notoriously, Ben Jonson labored to rescue his plays from the theatrical conditions in which they were produced, seeking to make available for readers a play text of which he could be said in some exact sense to be its "author." The 1600 quarto of *Every Man Out Of His Humor* insists on its title page (Fig. 2) that it presents the play "As It Was First Composed by the Author B. I. Containing more than hath been Publickely Spoken or Acted." Here Jonson asserts the authority of the literary text over the theatrical script, reversing the tendency to offer the play to a reading audience, in the familiar formula, "as it hath bene sundry times playd," as the 1600 quarto of *Henry V* (Fig. 3) has it. Even more remarkable is the 1605 quarto of *Sejanus*, to which Jonson contributes a preface in which he again announces that the printed text is "not the same with that which was acted on the publike stage." But in the published quarto, rather than merely restoring theatrical cuts, he has in fact removed and rewritten the work of a collaborator. While admitting that "A second pen had a good share" in what was played, in the printed text Jonson replaces the work of his unnamed co-author with his own words never acted, disingenuously claiming that his motive in inserting his own "weaker (and no doubt lesse pleasing)" language was only a reluctance "to defraud so happy a *Genius* of his right, by my lothed vsurpation" (sig. ¶2ʳ).

But if Jonson's aggressive determination to extract his plays from the customary collaborations of the theater is unique, his desire for a printed text that will preserve the dramatist's intended form is not. Other playwrights similarly saw print as the medium in which their intentions could be made visible at least to their readers. In the 1623 quarto of *The Duchess of Malfi*, Webster adds an anxious marginal note next to the italic text of a song sung by the churchmen in act three: "The Author disclaimes this Ditty to

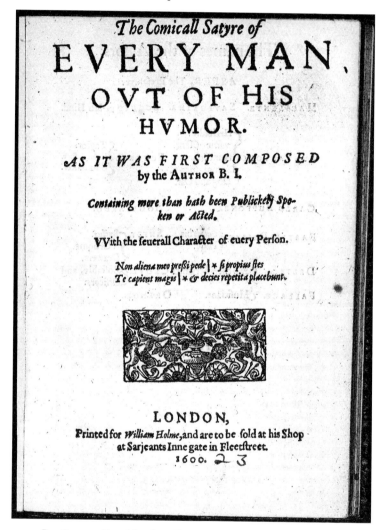

The Comicall Satyre of

EVERY MAN,

OVT OF HIS

HVMOR.

AS IT WAS FIRST COMPOSED
by the AUTHOR B. I.

Containing more than hath been Publickely Spo-
ken or Acted.

VVith the feuerall Character of euery Perfon.

Non aliena meo preſſi pede | ✳ ſi propius ſtes
Te capient magis | ✳ & decies repetita placebunt.

LONDON,
Printed for *William Holme,* and are to be fold at his Shop
at Sarjeants Inne gate in Fleetſtreet.
1600. 2 3

2. Ben Jonson, *Every Man Out of his Humor* (1600), title page, STC 14767

3. *Henry V* (1600), title page, STC 22289

be his" (sig. H2^r). More positive in its use of print is Barnabe Barnes's *The Devil's Charter* (1607), which advertises itself conventionally on the title page that it is presented "as it was plaide before the Kings Maiestie, upon Candlemasse night laste: by his Maiesties Servants," and then adds: "But more exactly revewed, corrected, and augmented since by the Author, for the more pleasure and profit of the Reader." A year later, Thomas Heywood insists in his epistle "To the Reader" in his *Rape of Lucrece* that it has not been "my custome . . . to commit my plaies to the presse"; nonetheless, on account of the copies that have "accidently come into the Printers handes" in "corrupt and mangled" form, "This therefore I was the willinger to furnish out in his natiue habit" (sig. A2ʳ). In 1640, Richard Brome adds an epistle to *The Antipodes* in which the "Curteous Reader" is told that this playbook, too, contains "more than was presented upon the *Stage*," where "for superfluous length (as some of the *Players* pretended)," cuts were made. Brome says that for this printed edition he thought it "good al should be inserted according to the allowed *Original*; and as it was, at first, intended for the *Cock-pit Stage*" (sig. L4ᵛ). For Brome, as for Heywood and Barnes, print restores and preserves the play he wrote, and, incidentally, his remarks reveal that it was the uncut, authorial text that was "allowed" by the Master of the Revels.

Shakespeare, however, never asserted any such proprietary right over his scripts or expressed any anxiety about their printed form. His plays, of course, were subjected to theatrical necessities, revised by various hands to allow them to play successfully within the two hours traffic of his stage, but never did Shakespeare feel obliged to "furnish" the play he wrote in its "natiue habit." Somewhat less than half of his dramatic output ever appeared in print while he lived, and of the plays that were published none is marked by any effort on his part to insure that the printed play accurately reflected what he had written. In their epistle "to the great Variety of Readers" in the 1623 folio, Heminge and Condell tell the would-be purchasers of the volume that the collection contains Shakespeare's plays exactly "as he conceiued the[m]," but that extravagant claim is never one Shakespeare felt inspired to make himself about any printed edition of his work.

Only eighteen of his thirty-seven plays were published in his lifetime, and none in an edition that Shakespeare avowed as his own. Still, with ten reprinted one or more times, at least forty-two separate editions reached print before he died. (If one counts *The Taming of A Shrew* as Shakespeare's, there are forty-five surviving editions of nineteen plays.) Clearly Shakespeare's plays were successful not only in the theater but also in the bookstalls, where they found a substantial reading audience. The first part of *Henry IV* appeared in six editions before his death, and a seventh before the folio was published in 1623. *Richard II* was published five times, as was *Richard III*. Several other plays were reprinted three times. At the time of his death, the total number of editions of Shakespeare's plays far exceeded that of any other contemporary playwright, and indeed no single play to that time had sold as well as *1 Henry IV*. (Even if one extends the time frame to 1640, only three plays – the anonymous *Mucedorus*, Kyd's *Spanish Tragedy*, and Marlowe's *Dr. Faustus* – appear in more editions than *1 Henry IV*'s seven, *Mucedorus*, somewhat improbably to modern taste, topping the list with fourteen printings between 1598 and 1639.)

While he lived, Shakespeare arguably had some competitors for theatrical preeminence, but what has often been overlooked is that as a published dramatist he had none. In our various measures of Shakespeare's greatness, we have usually ignored the fact that in his own age more editions of his plays circulated than of any other contemporary playwright. Eventually the prolific Beaumont and Fletcher would close the gap, but they never actually surpassed Shakespeare. Ironically, although he never sought his success as in print, he is the period's leading published playwright.

The reason that this has not been observed may be that print has seemed to many an inauthentic calculus of Shakespeare's achievement, but more likely it is simply that this success literally "goes without saying"; it appears to us inevitable that Shakespeare's plays would reach print and thrive in that medium. In his own time, however, that success was hardly assured. We see the drama as the most compelling cultural manifestation of the age and Shakespeare as its most extraordinary figure, but Shakespeare wrote in an environment in which plays, at least English plays, had not yet emerged as a literary genre; they were much like film scripts in the movie industry today. Publishers did not rush to publish new plays, largely because there was not a large and reliable market for them. Although William Prynne, in 1633, disgustedly insisted that playbooks were "now more vendible than the choicest sermons," claiming that "above forty thousand Play-bookes have beene printed and vented within these two years,"[2] even by his tendentious accounting, plays still represented only a small percentage of the books that were purchased. In the 1630s, booksellers sold something like twenty times as many religious books (sermons, catechisms, bibles, and theological works) as they did plays.[3]

Peter Blayney has usefully reminded us of what is all too easy to forget, given history's judgments on the period's cultural achievement: plays, even Shakespeare's plays, were a relatively insignificant piece of the book trade. They were at best a risky publishing venture. "No more than one play in five would have returned the publisher's initial investment inside five years," Blayney tells us, and "not one in twenty would have paid for itself during its first year."[4] While Shakespeare provided some publishers with considerable profit, eight of the eighteen plays that appeared in his lifetime did not merit a second edition before he died. And it is worth remembering that *Venus and Adonis* was published in sixteen editions by 1636, seven more than even the most successful of his plays.

In spite of the literary ambitions of some playwrights, printed plays were generally considered ephemera, among the "rifferaffes" and "baggage books" that Thomas Bodley would not allow in his library lest some "scandal" attach to it by their presence.[5] Publishers did regularly assume the risk of printing plays (though, between 1590 and 1615, on average only about ten were published a year), but they could not have done so imagining either that they were preserving the nation's cultural heritage or about to make their own fortune.

Plays were published in essence because they could be. In a commercial environment where publishing was largely opportunistic, plays were for a publisher a relatively inexpensive investment. If they did not, as Blayney says, offer a reliable "shortcut to wealth" (p. 389), they did allow a publisher the chance to make some money without great financial exposure. Manuscripts became available, probably at a cost to the publisher of no more than two pounds a piece. No record of any payment for a play survives, but evidence like that from the *Second Part of the Return From Parnassus*, where the printer John Danter (of whom more later) is imagined offering an author "40 shillings and an odde pottle of wine" for a manuscript, suggests that this was something like the going rate for a small book.[6] The play text would usually be printed in small pica type on nine sheets of the cheapest available paper. For an edition of 800, which was probably all a publisher would risk, the total costs of copy, registration, and printing would be about eight pounds. With playbooks retailing at around 6d. (viz., the "testerne" the publishers of the 1609 *Troilus and Cressida* hope its readers will think "well bestowd" with the play's purchase) and wholesaling at 4d., a publisher, especially one who sold his own books, could break even with the sale of about 500 copies and might then begin to turn a modest profit, which would average about a pound a year – certainly not a spectacular windfall but not an insubstantial contribution to the financial health of the stationer's business.[7]

"What made the venture worth the risk," writes Blayney, "was the chance that a well-chosen play would merit a second edition," which, because of its freedom from costs accruing only to the first (the price of the manuscript, entry, license, and registration), would nearly double the publisher's profit on wholesale copies (Blayney, p. 412). Interestingly, of plays first printed before 1625, almost half eventually appeared in a second edition (and about sixty per cent of those did so within ten years of the first date of publication), while for those first published after 1625, the number of plays appearing in two or more editions drops to ten per cent.[8] But even with the significant increase in profitability for individual copies of editions beyond the first, and, at least before 1625, with the substantial number of plays that were reprinted (allowing some amendment of Blayney's bleak accounting), no fortunes were made through play publication.

Of course, many plays never reached print at all. Those that did, almost certainly less than a fifth of the number played, arrived at their publishers from a variety of sources, and in the absence of anything like our modern copyright law, the publishers had no obligation to inquire scrupulously into their provenance. All that was legally required to establish title was that they not violate another stationer's claim to the text and that they follow the proper channels of authority in securing their right. If there was no prior claim, a publisher was free to print his copy with no regard for its author's rights or interests. As George Wither wrote in 1624: "by the lawes and Orders of their Corporation, they can and do setle vpon the particular members thereof p[e]rpetuall interest in such Bookes as are Registred by them at their Hall . . . notwithstanding their first Coppies were purloyned from the true owner, or imprinted without his leaue."

Until the first modern copyright law was passed in 1709, this remained the case. Copyright belonged to the publisher not to the author, and the legal situation, as Wither bitterly noted, served the publisher's interest at the expense of that of both the author and the reading public: "If he gett any written Coppy into his powre, likely to be vendible; whether the Author be willing or no, he will publish it; and it shallbe contriued and named alsoe, according to his owne pleasure: which is the reason, so many good Bookes come forth imperfect, and with foolish titles."[9]

Wither's account of the stationer's statutory freedom "to belye his Authors intentions" (sig. H5ʳ) is largely correct, though, in fairness, most stationers did make reasonable attempts to produce an accurate text. Authors, of course, regularly protested the failures of the printing house, as in Thomas Heywood's well-known complaint against "the infinite faults escaped in my book of *Britaines Troy* by the negligence of the printer, as the misquotations, mistaking of sillables, misplacing halfe lines, coining of strange and neuer heard of words. These being without number, when I would haue taken a particular account of the *Errata*, the printer answered me, he would not publish his owne disworkemanship, but rather let his owne fault lye vpon the necke of the Author."[10] But such charges also drew predictable replies from the stationers, who had to work quickly and often in circumstances that militated against precision, as John Windet insisted in a preliminary to a work of biblical commentary that he printed: "Some things haue escaped, others beene mistaken, partly by the absence of him who penned this Treatise, partly by the unleageableness of his hand in the written coppy."[11]

But Wither's main accusation, at least with regard to the drama, is true. Stationers for the most part showed little interest in either the quality or the origin of the dramatic texts they printed; they cared mainly that it be "vendible." Textual scholars, the heirs of Wither's dismay, have often used this fact to motivate their narratives of the transmission of Shakespeare's text. They similarly have stigmatized the stationers, or at least some, as dishonest and incompetent, all too willing to attempt a quick profit by publishing a pirated text of a play. But in truth the pirates, as Blayney and Laurie Maguire, among

others, have recently reminded us, are largely bogeys of our imagination, functions of an anachronistic understanding of both the
playhouse and the printing house.[12] This is not to say that publishers did inevitably purchase their copy from the author or some other
apparently legitimate owner; it is, however, to emphasize that stationers knew that the author's permission was not necessary to
publish the work, and knew as well that in the case of drama the very
notion of authorship is problematic. In any precise sense, the only
pirates, and there were some, were those publishers who undertook
to print a book that properly belonged to another stationer.

Unquestionably plays were often published without their
authors' consent or even knowledge, and in forms of which no
doubt their playwrights would never have approved; but this
should not be taken as anything more than evidence of the usual
– and fully legal – procedures of the contemporary book trade. A
potential publisher would purchase a manuscript of a play, which
might in some cases be authorial, though it could as well be a
scribal copy made for the acting company or for a collector, or a
transcript made by one or more actors. For the potential publisher
it made no difference; no one of these granted the publisher any
clearer authority over the text. All he would have been concerned
with was that the manuscript not cost too much, that it be reasonably legible, and that no other stationer have a claim to the play.

There are some examples of writers objecting to the publication
of defective versions of their work, although these inevitably reveal
how limited their ability was to oppose unauthorized publication.
Usually the most they could do was provide authorized copy to
replace the unsanctioned printing. Thus, Samuel Daniel explains
the publication of the second edition of his *Vision of the Twelve
Goddesses* in his dedication to the Countess of Bedford:

> *Madame*: In respect of the vnmannerly presumption of an indiscreet
> Printer, who without warrant hath divulged the late shewe at Court, . . .
> I thought it not amisse seeing it would otherwise passe abroad to the prej-
> udice both of the Maske and the inuention, to describe the whole forme
> thereof in all points as it was then performed . . .[13]

Similarly, Stephen Egerton, in a preface to the second edition of
one of his sermons that had been taken down by a listener in

shorthand, says that had it been his own doing originally he would have "beene more carefull in the manner of handling . . . And therefore that which I now do, is rather somewhat to qualifie an errour that cannot be recalled, then to publish a worke that may be in any way greatly commodious to other."[14] Both Daniel and Egerton are frustrated by the deficient texts that were published, but neither assumes that the publication of an unauthorized text is a legal issue. In the face of the publication of texts that neither author either delivered to or saw through the press, both realize that they have little recourse except to provide a better text for a new edition.

Regardless of the title page claims, playbooks were often unauthorized, published, that is, in editions that differed not only from the author's intended text but even from the text as it had been reshaped in performance; but these were not *illegal* printings. They do not provide evidence of criminal or dishonest business practices. Indeed this is true even for the so-called "bad quartos" of Shakespeare's plays. While these editions differ substantially from the familiar versions in which we know the play, and are arguably inferior if not corrupt, there is nothing to suggest their publishers knew them so. They operated in these cases very much as they did in all other publishing ventures, purchasing a play text on which they thought they might make a profit by having it printed and sold.

A published play text, we should remember, was not a priceless literary relic but a cheap pamphlet; it represented not the immortal words of a great writer but the work of professional actors whose skill involved improvisation as much as recall. The play itself had various lives in different theatrical venues, each of which would enforce changes upon the text. Why then would a publisher ever think in terms of the reliability or authority of the text?

Yet even if, however improbably, a publisher did so think, how would he recognize textual corruption? We hear a mangled phrase from a bad quarto, and our familiarity with the received text instantly reveals the deficiency. "To be, or not to be, I there's the point." There is no more familiar or compelling evidence of the manifest deficiency of Q1 *Hamlet* (sig. D4^v). But if we did not know the more familiar version would we think the line flawed? And indeed the putative corruption – "I there's the point" – is of course a perfectly uncorrupt Shakespearean line. It appears in *Othello*, after Othello painfully comes to see that his worst fears about Desdemona's betrayal must be true, revealingly in language that shows how fully he has internalized the pernicious racism that Iago exploits: "And yet how Nature erring from it selfe." Iago instantly interrupts, determined that there should be no retreat from the damning knowledge: "I, there's the point" (3.3.231–2, TLN 1854–5). In *Othello*, the line marks a moment of unmistakably Shakespearean power along the tragic trajectory of the play; in *Hamlet* it marks the corruption of the text.

The example may be too neat, and in truth when one looks at the whole speech in Q1 *Hamlet* one does find unmistakable signs of logical and syntactic jumble that seem more a function of the troubled transmission of the text than of the troubled mindset of its hero. Nonetheless, the initial question stands. Would a publisher who has come into possession of Q1 have any reason to be suspicious of the text he had purchased? At least at the level of text, the answer I would insist is "no," though with *Hamlet* there is another factor that complicates the issue. (I suppose with *Hamlet* there is always another factor that complicates the issue.)

Q1 *Hamlet* was published by Nicholas Ling and John Trundle in 1603; the play, however, had been registered to James Roberts on 26 July 1602. If the quality of the text was not unduly strained, the quality of their right to it seems to be. Roberts's entry establishes his title to the play, a title that is apparently violated by the edition that Ling and Trundle publish. Ling and Trundle are in this case perhaps truly pirates, not because they print a text in unauthorized form or one that had come to them via some actor but because they print a text registered to another stationer.

Nonetheless, I wonder if the ease with which we attribute piracy here is not more a function of our textual expectations than of its publishing history. The usual account is that Ling and Trundle have indeed published what Fredson Bowers calls "a memorially reconstructed pirate text."[15] A second quarto was, of course, published late in 1604, "Printed by I. R. for N. L.," as its title page has it (Fig. 4), that is, printed by James Roberts for Nicholas Ling. This quarto announces itself as "Newly imprinted and enlarged to

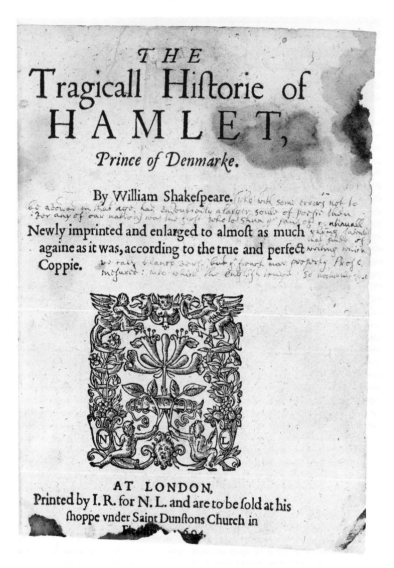

THE
Tragicall Hiftorie of
HAMLET,
Prince of Denmarke.

By William Shakefpeare.

Newly imprinted and enlarged to almoft as much
againe as it was, according to the true and perfect
Coppie.

AT LONDON,
Printed by I. R. for N. L. and are to be fold at his
fhoppe vnder Saint Dunftons Church in

4. Q2 *Hamlet* (1604), title page, STC 22276

almost as much againe as it was, according to the true and perfect Coppie." It is consciously designed to supplant the first, offering itself as new and improved, or, actually, new and restored, some 1,600 lines longer than Q1. The deficiencies of the earlier text are here replaced by authorized copy. Trundle's absence from the publishing arrangements of the second quarto have been taken as evidence that he was the supplier of the corrupt copy for Q1, and the co-operation of Roberts and Ling is seen as a pragmatic compromise that acknowledges Roberts's *de jure* title and Ling's *de facto* right. In the familiar textual history, Q2 marks the victory of truth and justice. The "memorially reconstructed pirate text" is replaced by a properly authorial version, and the rights of the abused stationer are restored.[16]

It is a good story, but it is not necessarily or even very probably true. Roberts, who was a printer rather than a publisher, had on numerous occasions entered material that was eventually published by another stationer but that Roberts himself printed. The entries seem to be for him usually a way of reserving work for himself without risking the capital that publication would involve. Roberts, for example, entered *The Merchant of Venice* in 1598, and two years later printed it for its eventual publisher, Thomas Hayes. Ling, on the other hand, was a publisher who, as Gerald Johnson has written, characteristically depended on "other stationers who located copy and brought it to him for help in publishing the editions," often with the printing job reserved for them as their reward.[17] Ling and Roberts also were well known to one another; twenty-three editions published by Ling came from Roberts's press. (Trundle, too, had employed Roberts, indeed in the very year that Q1 *Hamlet* was published.[18]) And title to *Hamlet* seems to have unproblematically settled on Ling, since he transfers it without question to John Smethwick in 1607.

Given these relationships, what seems most likely is that the publication of Q1 *Hamlet* was less piratical than pragmatic, the result of a rather ordinary set of prudent arrangements between stationers. The only thing that fits uncomfortably with this thesis is that Roberts did not in fact get to print Q1 *Hamlet*. It is, however, not unlikely that the traffic in his print shop (it was the third busiest year of Roberts's career in terms of the number of books printed and probably the heaviest measured by sheets printed) made it impossible to accept the job when it came due. For us it may seem incredible that a printer would pass up the opportunity to work on *Hamlet*, but job schedules would override any literary considerations; and, in any case, many things for a printer in 1603 might have seemed more compelling than a six-penny playbook, perhaps the edition of Drayton's *Barons' Wars* that Roberts printed that year for Ling, or Harsnett's *Declaration of Egregious Popish Impostures*, or even the two Bills of Mortality that he printed in the autumn of the year. Only an anachronistic sense of *Hamlet*'s value to a printer in 1603 has prevented the more likely version of events from being widely accepted. The putative corruptions of the text, the distortions of Shakespeare's great artistry, demand narratives of motivated villainy. Only a cad would publish a text as "bad" as Q1 *Hamlet*.

But to return to my major point here, it is not obvious to me that Ling and Trundle had any particular reason to think the text they published "bad" – or indeed any to think it particularly good. What they thought was that they had acquired copy that was "vendible," a play text that might be published with some small profit to them. When a new text became available the following year, supplied perhaps by the acting company who might well have been dismayed by what was in print, they were no doubt delighted to produce a second edition that might inspire new sales. This is a less interesting story, I admit, than tales of pirates, but it is almost certainly closer to the truth.

I am not saying that Q1 *Hamlet* is as good a play as the *Hamlet* that we usually read (though I would say that it is a better play than has generally been allowed, and certainly not "*Hamlet* by Dogberry," as Brian Vickers has termed it[19]); I am saying only that such questions of literary judgment should not be allowed to color our understanding of the textual history. When we see that history backwards, through the filter of a cultural authority not fully achieved until the mid-eighteenth century, inevitably we get it wrong. Shakespeare, one could say, was not exactly Shakespeare during his own lifetime.

An obvious example: when his plays were first published, his name was not what distinguished them in the bookstalls. As is well known, eight of Shakespeare's plays were published over four years before one appeared in print with his name on the title page. Cuthbert Burby first included Shakespeare's name on the quarto of *Love's Labor's Lost* (Fig. 5) in 1598, and even then hardly as a ringing affirmation of authorship, the title page asserting only that the play was "Newly corrected and augmented *By W. Shakespere*," the name set in small italic type. Previously editions of *Titus Andronicus*, *2* and *3 Henry VI*, *The Taming of the Shrew*, *Romeo and Juliet*, *Richard II*, *Richard III*, and *1 Henry IV*, had all been published with no indication that Shakespeare was the playwright. The plays, with the exception of *2 Henry VI*, all advertise the authority of the text as theatrical rather than authorial, by insisting that it is published "As it was Plaide."

One should, of course, conclude that what this means is that before 1598 the name "Shakespeare" on the title page was not yet seen as sufficient inducement for a potential customer to purchase a play text at a bookstall. Indeed, most published plays advertised their theatrical auspices, emphasizing for us yet again that the drama was still subliterary, its audience, even for the published play, understood primarily as theater-goers. The six-penny pamphlets were a relatively cheap way of happily recalling a performance or catching up with one that had unhappily been missed. Richard Hawkins reminds the potential buyers of his edition of *Philaster* (1628) that the play "was affectionately taken, and approoved by the Seeing Auditors, or Hearing Spectators (of which sort I take, or conceive you to be the greatest part)," though he anticipates also that his edition will be "eagerly sought for, not onely by those that haue heard & seene it, but by others that haue merely heard therof" (sig. A2ᵛ).

As excitement about a production waned with time, however, the published play would normally become less marketable: "When they grow stale they must be vented by Termers and Cuntrie chapmen," says Middleton in his preface to *The Family of Love* (1608), distressed that publication of his play had not taken place "when the newnesse of it made it much more desired" (sig. A1ᵛ). Printed plays do seem for the most part to be tied to theatrical success, published with the hope, as Brome says in his epistle to *The Antipodes*, that "the publicke view of the world entertayn it with no lesse welcome, then that private one of the stage already has

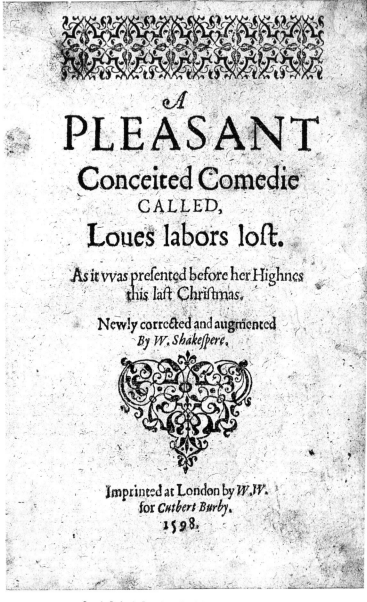

A
PLEASANT
Conceited Comedie
CALLED,
Loues labors loft.

As it vvas prefented before her Highnes
this laft Chriftmas.

Newly correfted and augmented
By *W. Shakefpere.*

Imprinted at London by *W.W.*
for *Cutbert Burby.*
1598.

5. *Love's Labor's Lost* (1598), title page, STC 22294

given it" (sig. A2ᵛ); or, as Heywood writes in his preface to *Greene's Tu quoque* (1614): "since it hath past the Test of the stage with so generall an applause, pitty it were but it should likewise haue the honour of the Presse" (sig. A2ʳ).

The "honour of the Presse" was usually reserved for plays that had succeeded on stage (*Troilus and Cressida* and *The Knight of the Burning Pestle* are the notable exceptions, for each the dramatic failure functioning as a sign of its sophistication[20]); and not surprisingly, then, title pages usually advertised their plays as the records of performance rather than as the registers of a literary intention. Whatever the actual status of the underlying manuscript, if the market for playbooks was largely playgoers then the strategy makes sense. Within a theatrical economy, display of an author's name on a play text offered no particular commercial advantage. It does seem, however, that, at least in Shakespeare's case, this was in the process of changing. In 1598, reprints of both *Richard II* and *Richard III* were published that did include Shakespeare's name on the title page, and in 1599, a new edition of *1 Henry IV* was reissued with Shakespeare's name added. In the remaining years before Shakespeare died, twenty-nine editions of eighteen separate plays were published, only eight of which appeared without identifying Shakespeare as the playwright.

Most remarkable in this regard is the edition of *King Lear* published by Nathaniel Butter in 1608, with a title page (Fig. 6) not merely identifying Shakespeare as the playwright but trumpeting his authorship at the head of the page and in a larger typeface than had ever before been used for his name: "M. William Shak-speare: / HIS / True Chronicle Historie of the life and / death of King LEAR and his three / Daughters." Here the play is displayed and celebrated as Shakespeare's, but the printed text is no more exclusively "HIS" than any of the other published plays that had previously escaped his control. It is a poorly printed play (indeed the first that its printer, Nicholas Okes, had ever undertaken), and Shakespeare did not oversee its publication or concern himself with the imperfect results.

The play is obviously presented as Shakespeare's, but it literally belongs to Butter, the publisher who owns and controls the text, asserting Shakespeare's authorship as a marketing strategy, both to

M. William Shak-ſpeare:

HIS

True Chronicle Hiſtorie of the life and
death of King L ᴇ ᴀ ʀ and his three
Daughters.

With the vnfortunate life of Edgar, *ſonne*
and heire to the Earle of Gloſter, and his
ſullen and aſſumed humor of
Toᴍ of Bedlam :

*As it was played before the Kings Maieſtie at Whitehall vpon
S.* Stephans *night in Chriſtmas Hollidayes.*

By his Maieſties ſeruants playing vſually at the Gloabe
on the Bancke-ſide.

LONDON,
Printed for *Nathaniel Butter,* and are to be ſold at his ſhop in *Pauls*
Church-yard at the ſigne of the Pide Bull neere
Sᵗ. *Auſtins* Gate. 1 6 0 8

6. *King Lear* (1608), title page, STC 22292

capitalize on Shakespeare's reputation and to differentiate this play from an anonymous play text of 1605, *The True Chronicle History of King Leir* (Fig. 7). Shakespeare's name functions on the 1608 title page perhaps as much to identify the play*book* as the play*wright*. In either role, of course, it serves as a mark of distinction, but Shakespeare is here always the publisher's Shakespeare, not the author himself, a simulacrum invented to protect and promote the publisher's property.[21]

The 1608 *Lear* quarto, then, does at least seem to point to Shakespeare's growing literary reputation. Butter, though he is unconcerned to provide a carefully printed text, is eager to offer what he publishes as Shakespeare's play and not merely as the record of performance by the King's men. Here is the earliest incontrovertible evidence of what in 1622 Thomas Walkley would claim in his edition of *Othello* (1622): that "The Authors name is sufficient to vent his work." Certainly Butter believed this true, publishing in 1605 an edition of *The London Prodigall* with a title page (Fig. 8) claiming that it is "By William Shakespeare." We cannot know whether or not Butter thought the play was in fact by Shakespeare, but obviously he thought Shakespeare's name would help sell the playbook.

And other publishers apparently thought similarly. The two parts of *The Troublesome Raigne of King John* were published first in 1591 by Sampson Clarke with no authorial attribution but rather with the familiar title page statement that the play was set forth "As it was (sundry times) publikely acted by the Queenes Maiesties Players" (Fig. 9); but when it was reprinted in 1611 by John Helme, the title page, while announcing that the text was offered "As it was sundry times lately acted by the Queenes Maiesties Players" ("lately" replacing "publikely," as the Queen's men were then defunct), now included a new – and seemingly inaccurate – assertion that the two parts were "Written by W. Sh."[22] And when it was again reprinted in 1622, this time by Thomas Dewe, the name of the acting company had disappeared from the assertion that it was "(sundry times) lately acted" and the title page proudly claimed it was "Written by W. Shakespeare" (Fig. 10). For Helme and Dewe it may merely be that they assumed this play was indeed Shakespeare's *King John*; in any case, it seems likely that it was the

THE
True Chronicle Hi-
ſtory of King LEIR, and his three
daughters, *Gonorill, Ragan,*
and *Cordella.*

As it hath bene diuers and ſundry
times lately acted.

LONDON,

Printed by Simon Stafford for Iohn
Wright, and are to bee ſold at his ſhop at
Chriſtes Church dore, next Newgate-
Market. 1 6 0 5.

7. *King Leir* (1605), title page, STC 5343

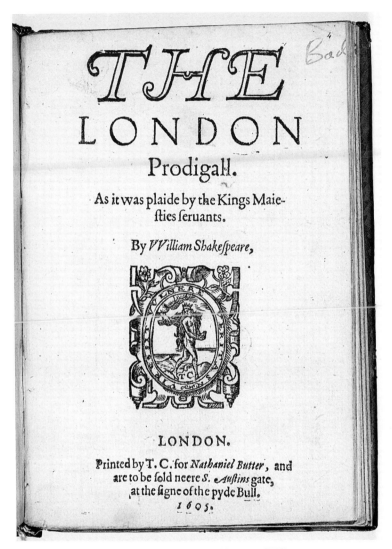

THE
LONDON
Prodigall.

As it was plaide by the Kings Maie-
fties feruants.

By *VVilliam Shakefpeare,*

LONDON.

Printed by T. C. for *Nathaniel Butter*, and
are to be fold neere *S. Auftins* gate,
at the figne of the pyde Bull.
1605.

8. *The London Prodigal* (1605), title page, STC 22333

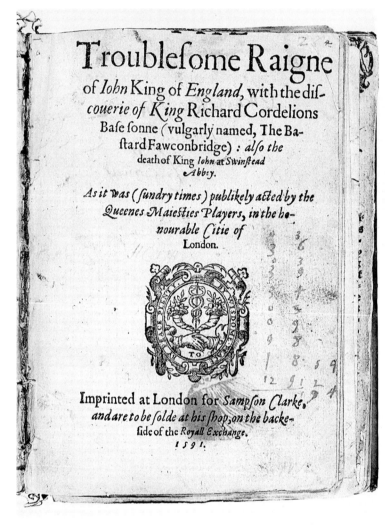

9. *The Troublesome Reign of King John* (1591), title page, STC 14644

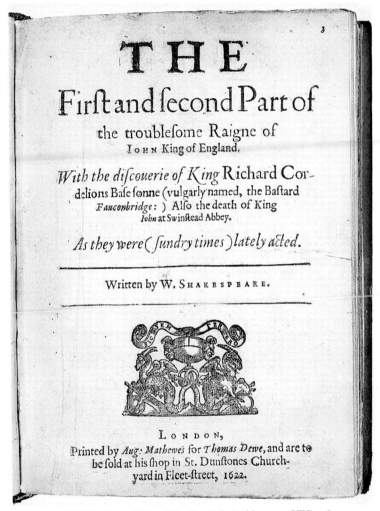

THE

First and second Part of

the troublesome Raigne of
I O H N King of England.

With the discouerie of King Richard Cor-
delions Base sonne (vulgarly named, the Bastard
Fauconbridge:) Also the death of King
John at Swinstead Abbey.

As they were (sundry times) lately acted.

Written by W. S H A K E S P E A R E.

L O N D O N,
Printed by *Aug: Mathewes* for *Thomas Dewe*, and are to
be fold at his shop in St. Dunstones Church-
yard in Fleet-street, 1622.

10. *The Troublesome Reign of King John* (1622), title page, STC 14647

rights to *The Troublesome Raigne* that were leased by the consortium that published the Shakespeare folio, since the yet unpublished Shakespearean *King John* was not among the sixteen plays "not formerly entred to other men" duly registered by Jaggard and Blount on 8 November 1623. Yet, whatever the publishers' understanding about the play's authorship, what is absolutely clear is that year by year on the bookstalls the commercial cachet of an old acting company weakened, while the commercial cachet of an old playwright grew.

But if some publishers were indeed convinced that "Shakespeare" on the title page would help sell books, others seemed less certain about the marketability of the playwright's name. *Titus Andronicus*, for example, was published in 1594 with no indication of its author, only that it had been "Plaide by the Right Honourable the Earle of *Darbie*, Earle of *Pembrooke*, and Earle of *Sussex* their servaunts." The reticence about authorship here was no doubt because in 1594 the theatrical provenance of the play was more impressive than its still little-known author; but the play was reissued two more times after its first printing (once in 1600 and again in 1611), with title pages that carefully updated its theatrical history but each still with no acknowledgement that Shakespeare was its author.

Similarly, in 1599, Cuthbert Burby published the second edition of *Romeo and Juliet* (Fig. 11), but that title page gives no indication that the play was by Shakespeare; and, lest this be taken only as evidence that even by 1599 the value of Shakespeare's name was still being negotiated, ten years later *Romeo and Juliet*, like *Titus*, was published again, still without identifying Shakespeare as the playwright. And indeed about eleven years after that, roughly the time when Thomas Walkley was insisting upon the commercial value of Shakespeare's name, yet another edition of *Romeo and Juliet* (Q4) appeared, which again failed to identify its author (Fig. 12) – though interestingly a variant title page was issued that does claim the play was "Written by *W. Shake-speare*" (Fig. 13).[23]

This edition (with its two separate title pages) was published by John Smethwick, who, on the basis of the titles he controlled, apparently was invited in as a minor partner in the consortium of stationers who combined to publish the first folio. I take it that

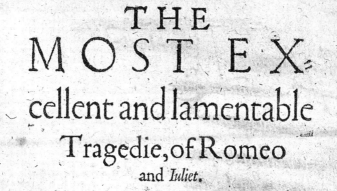

THE
MOST EX-
cellent and lamentable
Tragedie, of Romeo
and *Iuliet*.

*Newly corrected, augmented, and
amended:*

As it hath bene sundry times publiquely acted, by the
right Honourable the Lord Chamberlaine
his Seruants.

LONDON
Printed by Thomas Creede, for Cuthbert Burby, and are to
be sold at his shop neare the Exchange.
1599.

11. *Romeo and Juliet* (1599), title page, STC 22323

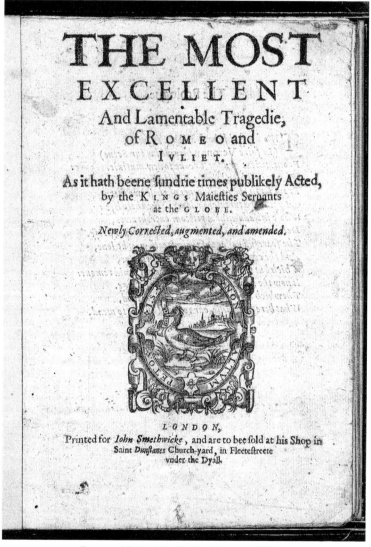

THE MOST
EXCELLENT
And Lamentable Tragedie,
of R o m e o and
I v l i e t.

As it hath beene ſundrie times publikely Acted,
by the K i n g s Maieſties Seruants
at the G l o b e.

Newly Corrected, augmented, and amended.

LONDON,
Printed for *Iohn Smethwicke*, and are to bee ſold at his Shop in
Saint *Dunſtanes* Church-yard, in Fleeteſtreete
vnder the Dyall.

12. *Romeo and Juliet,* (1622?), Q4 title page, STC 22325

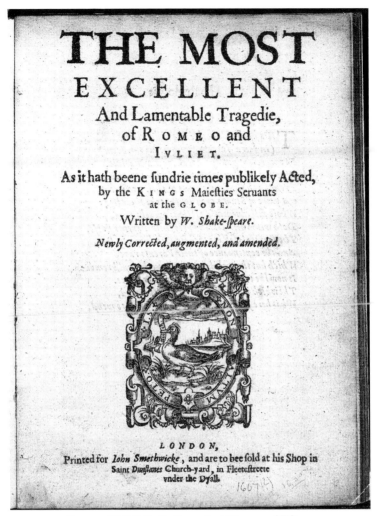

THE MOST
EXCELLENT
And Lamentable Tragedie,
of R o m e o and
I v l i e t.

As it hath beene sundrie times publikely Acted,
by the K i n g s Maiesties Seruants
at the G l o b e.

Written by *W. Shake-speare.*

Newly Corrected, augmented, and amended.

LONDON,
Printed for *Iohn Smethwicke*, and are to bee sold at his Shop in
Saint *Dunstanes* Church-yard, in Fleetestreete
vnder the Dyall.

13. *Romeo and Juliet* (1622?), Q4 variant title page, STC 22325a

Smethwick, who had acquired the rights to the play from Nicholas Ling in 1607, had prepared a new edition of *Romeo and Juliet*, a reprint of the 1609 printing, and issued it with a reset version of the earlier title page on which Shakespeare's name does not appear. The variant title page (with Shakespeare's name) seems almost certainly to have been printed later, most likely issued sometime after negotiations for the folio rights revealed to Smethwick the nature of his property. (It is very improbable that the authorial title page was issued first, as there is no obvious commercial reason to remove Shakespeare's name, but there is an obvious one to add it.) But until the issue of the variant title page of *Romeo and Juliet*, Smethwick, just like Edward White, the publisher of the later *Titus* quartos, had published two editions of the play he controlled without identifying either as Shakespeare's; and, though it may seem incredible to us, it is at least possible that Smethwick, like White, did so without knowing that Shakespeare was the author.

How this could be the case is instructive. Both plays were first published by John Danter, *Titus Andronicus* in 1594, the first of Shakespeare's plays to appear in print or at least the earliest surviving publication, and *Romeo and Juliet* in 1597. Danter was an active stationer in London in the 1590s before his death at age thirty-four in October 1599; in his eight-year career he printed or published seventy-nine editions of sixty-seven separate titles, mainly popular forms, like ballads, pamphlets, and plays. Danter's professional behavior, however, has been consistently denigrated as immoral and inept. E. K. Chambers, for example, identified Danter as "a stationer of the worst reputation," and R. B. McKerrow wrote of the 1597 *Romeo and Juliet* that "like all his work, it was very badly printed."[24] W. W. Greg agreed, combining the two judgments into general misgiving: "any dramatic quarto with which [Danter] was concerned is necessarily suspect in the first instance." Danter's career, Greg concludes, "is nothing but a record of piracy and secret printing."[25] For D. Allen Carroll, similarly, the whole career is tainted: "Everyone knows of the odor which attaches itself to the name of Danter."[26]

But this may be another case where our anachronistic hopes and expectations for Shakespeare's text have infected our historical judgment; "the odor which attaches itself to the name of Danter" may not be the fetid scent of fraudulence or incompetence but only the homely smell of workmanlike activity. Danter did find himself entangled in various difficulties with the Stationers' Company, but they were for the most part the sort of disputes that affected almost every member of the guild at one time or other. In 1586, Danter was one of six stationers accused of violating Francis Flower's patent to print *Accidence*, a popular Latin grammar, and with the others he was found guilty of illegal printing and "Dyshabled to prynte, otherwyse then as Iourneymen," as the Stationers' Court decreed; nonetheless in 1589 he was sworn and admitted a freeman of the company.[27] In 1593 arbitration was ordered for some unnamed conflict that Danter had with Henry Chettle and Cuthbert Burby, a dispute inconsequential enough, however, that the three men on and off continued to work with one another to the end of the decade. More seriously, in 1597, he had his presses and type "defaced and made vnservciable for pryntinge" for printing the *Jesus Psalter*, a work of Catholic devotion, "without aucthoritie."[28]

Danter's court record marks him as at worst a recusant but hardly a wicked or even particularly unruly stationer. In almost all regards, including the difficulties he gets into with the Company, he behaves very much like other members of the book trade. The animus that attaches to him results mainly from his publication of the "bad quarto" of *Romeo and Juliet* in 1597. It is that offence that is "rank" and "smells to heaven" – or at least to the acute olfactory sense of the new bibliographers. Danter is guilty of printing an imperfect text of one of Shakespeare's plays. There is no reason, of course, to think he knew it imperfect, and the printing itself is unremarkable, except that half way through the text the type font changes. Rather typically, the observation of this fact produces more derision: "never was a masterpiece ushered into the world in a worse manner," said Plomer,[29] but in truth the change in font reveals only that the printing was shared, probably with Edward Allde. Such shared printing was not uncommon (Dekker's *The Honest Whore* and the three 1604 quartos of *The Malcontent* are examples[30]), and typographically little marks the composition and presswork as defective, and indeed it is not in any sense a poorer printing job than Q2, the so-called "good quarto" of *Romeo and*

Juliet.[31] The play, however, was not registered by Danter, and the absence of an entry, coupled with a text that seems to have been adapted for performance and perhaps reconstructed by its actors, has led to its vilification, most recently by a scholar as normally judicious as David Bevington, who calls it "a pirated edition issued by an unscrupulous publisher."[32]

Danter's *Romeo and Juliet*, however, was not a "pirated edition," and neither the quality nor the provenance of the text can be used to prove its publisher "unscrupulous." Printing a play that had been abridged for performance or even one recalled and reassembled by its actors did not violate any law or regulation. No stationer had a prior claim to the text of *Romeo and Juliet*, and Danter's avoidance of the expected registration procedures may have been motivated by nothing more nefarious than his desire to save the required fees. His usual habits, it is worth noting, were more conventional. He was involved in the publication of nine plays, three of which he printed for other stationers; of the six he published himself, four were properly registered, including *Titus Andronicus*.

There is no particular reason to see his handling of *Romeo and Juliet* as symptomatic of some character flaw, or indeed as anything worse than somewhat cavalier treatment of what was essentially a pamphlet at a moment when his own career seemed to be in free fall. In 1595 he was involved with nineteen publications; in 1596, with eleven; in 1597, the year *Romeo and Juliet* was published, only three; the following year just one. Late that year or early the next he died, and in 1600 the Stationers' Company granted his widow and children "twentye Shillinge a yere . . . out of the poores Accoumpt," the mark of their poverty an addendum that an additional five shillings was "to be gyven vnto her presently in hand."[33] However *Romeo and Juliet* came into his possession, it must have seemed a small miracle. We might think better of Danter if we see his decision to save himself ten pence by denying the play both license and entrance less as an effort to put forth a degraded version of one of Shakespeare's tragedies than as one to put food on the table for his family.

In any case, *Romeo and Juliet* fared better than its publisher. By 1599 Danter was dead, his family destitute; that same year, Cuthbert Burby reissued the play in a new edition, "Newly Corrected,

Augmented, and Amended." Printed by Thomas Creede, this second quarto (which is about 700 lines longer than Q1) seems to have been printed from Shakespeare's papers, which must have been received directly from the acting company. This seems to be another occasion, like those involving Samuel Daniel or Stephen Egerton, where an effort was made to substitute an authorized text for one that was deemed deficient.

But, interestingly, however much the new edition of *Romeo and Juliet* was motivated by the desire to establish an *authorized text*, the effort does not involve the establishment of an *author*. Q2 may well be, as many bibliographers believe, a "good quarto" deriving from Shakespeare's own papers, but what should not be forgotten is that neither the publisher nor the supplier of the good text thought it useful to say so. The play is once again published by Burby as a performance text, printed "as it hath bene sundry time publiquely acted," though arguably that describes the theatrically abridged text of Q1 more accurately than it does Q2, which, deriving from the playwright's papers, seemingly deserves precisely what it is denied: the acknowledgement that it is by William Shakespeare.[34] Such acknowledgement, however, was not forthcoming.

Burby's receipt, in whatever manner, of Shakespeare's papers does not mark his edition as any more regular than Danter's. Indeed Burby's rights to the play most likely derive from some unrecorded negotiation with Danter. They had on occasion worked together. Danter had printed *The Cobbler's Prophecy* for Burby in 1594, and, more revealingly, the previous year Danter had entered the play *Orlando Furioso* and then transferred his title to Burby with the proviso, as the Stationers' Register records it, "(Danter to have the printing)." It is even possible that Burby's publication of *Love's Labor's Lost* similarly derives from a negotiation with Danter, who, it is plausible to think, may have printed the lost quarto that Burby's 1598 edition offers as "Newly corrected and augmented *By W. Shakespere.*" In any case, though unregistered, Burby's rights to *Romeo and Juliet* were unquestioned, and in 1607 he transferred his title to Nicholas Ling. Nine months later, Ling transferred the rights to *Romeo and Juliet*, along with fifteen other titles, to John Smethwick, who (as we have seen) printed an edition of the play in 1609, again advertising it as "Newly corrected, augmented, and amended" – though in fact the title page, like the text itself, is a simple reprint of Q2 – and again omitting the name of the playwright, as he did once more in 1622, until he decided to issue the variant title page.

Since its first appearance in 1597, then, the play had belonged to four men, none of whom had felt obligated by either bibliographic scruple or commercial consideration to acknowledge Shakespeare's authorship. As the play became a less familiar element in the repertory of the King's men (and indeed no record survives of any production after 1598), the recurring title page claim that the play was printed "as it hath beene sundrie times publiquely acted" inevitably became more gestural than descriptive, and as Shakespeare's name had become increasingly "vendible" in the marketplace of print, it is hard to imagine that if he was recognized as the play's author his name would not have been used to help sell the editions (as indeed it is on the variant 1622 title page).

But play texts, we must again remind ourselves, had not yet fully made the transition from the ephemera of an emerging entertainment industry to the artifacts of high culture. They did not yet demand an author, and in some sense they did not deserve one, the text being so fully a record of the collaborative activities of a theatrical company. As publishers transferred titles to such works there is no reason to think the author's name would automatically attach itself and follow along. Today we hear the title *Romeo and Juliet* and instantly supply Shakespeare's name. In 1597, in 1599, in 1609, and even in 1622, the Shakespearean canon did not yet firmly exist. The publishers who printed the play were arguably unaware, and certainly unimpressed, that they were printing a play by Shakespeare. In this regard it is worth noting that the Stationers' Register entry that records the transfer of titles from Ling to Smethwick has items like "Master DRAYTONs *Poemes*," "master GREENEs *Arcadia*," and "SMYTHs *common Wealth of England*"; the plays, however, are anonymous: "ROMEO and JULETT," "The Taminge of A Shrewe," "Loues Labour Lost," and "a booke called Hamlett."

Authorship is important to us, heirs of a romantic conception of writing as individual and originary, and if it was indeed important to some of Shakespeare's contemporaries, it was not particularly important to Shakespeare himself or to the publishers who first brought his plays to the reading public. In setting forth his plays, they did not see their task as the preservation of the work of the nation's greatest writer; they were seeking only some small profit with limited financial vulnerability, as with their six-penny pamphlets they turned Shakespeare into "a man in Print" and made his plays available to desiring readers.

CHAPTER TWO

From quarto to folio; or, size matters

His riper age
Requires a more misterious folio page.
Robert Fletcher, "The Publique Faith"

If there had been an opportunity for an additional title for the first chapter of this book, my fatal Cleopatra might well have led me to call it "Shakespeare by Accident," a pun designed to embrace both the casualness that surrounded the early publication of Shakespeare's plays and the actual typographic process of their materialization in the printing house; and if such multiple naming was any way encouraged, this present chapter might then have been titled "Dedicated Shakespeare." While publication of the quartos was for the most part opportunistic and haphazard, the publication in 1623 of the volume usually known as the first folio resulted only from the extraordinary dedication to the project by a number of people to produce what was in every sense a monumental book; and, of course, the book itself was literally dedicated – by Heminge and Condell to that "most noble and incomparable paire of brethren," William and Philip Herbert, earls of Pembroke and Montgomery respectively, consecrating to their Lordships "these remaines of your seruant Shakespeare" that are preserved in the volume and offered as a "present" made worthy "by the perfection." In their dedication, in both senses of the word, Heminge and Condell express "their gratitude both to the liuing, and the dead."

The folio was an impressive book, in almost every way different from the small, inexpensive, and quickly printed quartos that made their way to the bookstalls around St. Paul's, but most obviously distinguished by its size. To state the obvious: folios were big books, usually about fourteen inches high and nine inches wide (their actual size, of course, is not prescribed but a function of the fact that "folio" technically refers to a book made up of gatherings of sheets each folded once along the longer side to make two leaves or four pages; hence a folio page would normally be larger than anything other than the unfolded broadsheet, though, as sheets themselves came in various sizes, this would not necessarily be the case). The imposing physical stature of a folio book, and the attendant costs, made it appropriate only for consequential publications in subjects like theology or law.

There is no technical reason, of course, why anything could not be printed in folio, even an individual play, and indeed several were, most notably an edition of Suckling's *Aglaura* published in 1638, a tall, thin book of twenty-eight leaves. The oddity of a folio playbook, however, did not go unremarked. Richard Brome wrote a witty poem "Upon *Aglaura* Printed in Folio," finding the prodigal use of paper no less inappropriate than the eccentricity of the format. "This great voluminous Pamphlet may be said / To be like one who hath more haire then head," jokes Brome, and continues: "Should this new fashion last but one halfe year / Poets as Clarks would make our paper dear." To print a play in folio, Brome says, is "to lodge a Child in the great bed of Ware," and he ends: "Give me the sociable pocket books, / These empty folio's only please the Cooks."[1]

Brome's gibes were not prompted by any aspect of Suckling's dramaturgy but rather by the presumption of presenting it in folio. Size obviously does matter, at least in some contexts. And whether or not Suckling was abashed at the jests at his Brobdingnagian play publication, it is interesting to note that *Aglaura* was not reprinted in folio form, appearing again only in the various editions of Suckling's collected works, all of which were issued in octavo. *Aglaura*, then, reverses the bibliographic trajectory we are familiar with from Shakespeare, where small-format editions of single plays give way to the folio collection. At very least the example of Suckling reveals that more does not inevitably imply bigger.

It does, however, with Shakespeare, if only because thirty-six plays collected in a smaller format would produce an unattractively fat volume, substantially wider than it would be tall. As it is, however, the folio of 1623 is physically arresting, as is appropriate for the ambitions of the collection. With its more than 900 double-columned pages, an engraved portrait, prefatory epistles, and commendatory verse, it presents itself as a significant book, the product of much planning and labor. The complex, expensive, and time-consuming process of assembling rights and printing the texts of thirty-six plays itself argues a carefully designed and thoroughly motivated effort. Whose motivations these were, however, is not so obvious.

Whose motivations they *were not* is, however, perfectly clear. They were not Shakespeare's. He was dead. He had died in 1616, seven years before the folio appeared. His two friends and fellow actors, John Heminge and Henry Condell, who served, in their own phrase, to "gather his works," voice their disappointment that their labor is necessary, wishing that Shakespeare "had liu'd to haue set forth, and ouerseen his owne writings."

But even had he been alive there is no reason to think he would have agreed to do so. Shakespeare had never revealed any interest in publishing his plays, seemingly content to produce them for the theater alone. He never demonstrated anything like the extraordinary literary ambitions of Ben Jonson, but neither did he display even the more modest proprietary concerns of a playwright like Heywood, who consented "to commit [his] plaies to the presse," but only, or so he protests, to replace the "corrupt and mangled" texts that had "accidently come into the Printers hands."[2]

With whatever actual reluctance, Heywood and other contemporary playwrights repeatedly acknowledged that print offered them the opportunity to correct or at least apologize for the unauthorized plays that circulated. "A kinde of necessity enioyned" them, in Heywood's phrase, "to thrust into the Presse" plays intended only for the stage.[3] (And whether sincere or not, the very reiteration of the protest confirms that a play text was often considered, if only by its author, a form of intellectual property.) But no "necessity," it is worth repeating, ever "enioyned" Shakespeare to produce and oversee an authorized edition of any of his plays, a considerable number of which had been published in editions that had arrived at the print shop no less "accidently" and had left it in editions no less "corrupt and mangled" than those of which other dramatists regularly complained.

Nonetheless, in our desire for an authenticity the surviving texts deny us, we are reluctant to accept the evidence of his apparent lack of concern for their deficiencies. "It is foolish to suppose," writes W. W. Greg, "that Shakespeare was indifferent to the fate of his own work,"[4] though in truth nothing beyond the unactable length of some play texts can be educed to support Greg's supposition. And desire leads even the usually positivistic Greg to indulge in a fantasy of Shakespeare's literary ambition, as he wonders if Shakespeare did not "dream in his garden at Stratford of a great volume of his plays, such as his friend Jonson was busy preparing."[5]

No record of that dream survives (unless it is in the as yet undiscovered notes of the psychotherapist Shakespeare visits in *Shakespeare in Love*). Greg, I suspect, is projecting. It is quite possibly what he often dreamed of: an authorized edition. But Shakespeare's dreams are not available to us, and even Greg's are hardly compelling bibliographic evidence. Almost two centuries before Greg, Samuel Johnson had similarly thought about Shakespeare in his retirement in Stratford, but characteristically the sensible Johnson focused only on what Shakespeare did, or, in this case, did not do: "So careless was this great poet of future fame that, though he retired to ease and plenty, while he was yet little 'declined into the vale of years,' before he could be disgusted with fatigue, or disabled by infirmity, he made no collection of his works, nor desired to rescue those that had already been published from the depravations that obscured them, or secure to the rest a better destiny, by giving them to the world in their genuine state."[6]

Dr. Johnson observes what is seemingly unavoidable: that Shakespeare, with the leisure to have done otherwise, made no effort to collect and perfect the plays that had been published or that had remained with the acting company. Heminge and Condell indeed may have wished that Shakespeare had lived "*to be exequutor to his owne writings*," but in truth he had lived long enough to have overseen his plays and had not done anything to bring a collected volume into being. If Ben Jonson's plan for a folio was, as seems likely, known to Shakespeare, it did not stimulate in him any ambition to become an "author" like his friend. Everything suggests that Shakespeare could have said with Heywood – and more convincingly than that playwright who was regularly tempted by the promises of print – "it was neuer any great ambition in me, to bee in this kind Voluminously read."[7]

The project of the collected volume must have begun with Heminge and Condell themselves sometime after Shakespeare died. Leonard Digges, in a commendatory poem addressed to Shakespeare, extols the labor of the two "pious fellowes" who have given "The world thy Workes." And at least one other contemporary toasted their editorial activity, in a poem entitled "To my good freandes mr John Hemings & Henry Condall":

> To yowe that Joyntly with vndaunted paynes
> Vowtsafed to Chawnte to vs thease noble straynes,
> How mutch yowe merrytt by it, it is not sedd,
> But yowe haue pleased the lyving, loved the deadd,
> Raysde from the woamb of Earth a ritcher myne
> Than Curteys [i.e., Cortez] Cowlde with all his Castellyne
> Associattes, they dydd butt digg for Golwlde,
> Butt yowe for Treasure mutch moare manifollde.[8]

Their editorial work is imagined not in the conventional resurrection metaphor of memorial volumes; it is not the dead author who rises from the grave to live eternally in the volume of his works, but the treasure of the works themselves that is "Raysde from the woamb of Earth" by Heminge and Condell's "vndaunted paynes," a treasure that is thought greater than the riches of the new world. For both of the dedicatees of the volume, each with heavy investments in the Virginia company and other North American joint stock ventures, the comparison was perhaps not an entirely felicitous one.

Heminge and Condell had been associated with Shakespeare almost from the beginning of his establishment in the theatrical community, possibly from the very early years of the 1590s, when all three might have been involved with Lord Pembroke's men. Sometime later in the decade they were certainly all together in fellowship in Lord Hunsdon's company, which became the Lord Chamberlain's men upon Hunsdon's assumption of that position in March 1597. In 1616, when Shakespeare died, only three of the original shareholders in the company were still alive – Heminge, Condell, and Richard Burbage – and Shakespeare in his will left each 26s. 8d. to buy memorial rings. Five years later, by which time the planning for the folio must have been well underway, only Heminge and Condell still lived, Burbage having died on 13 March 1619.

Their role, then, as "Presenters," as they call themselves in the dedication, has an inevitability about it. They were the last survivors of the great age of Shakespeare, determined "to keepe the memory of so worthy a Friend, and Fellow, alive." Possibly prompted by the publication of Ben Jonson's works in 1616, and provoked by the effort in 1619 of Thomas Pavier and William Jaggard to publish a collection of Shakespeare's plays, they conceived the project; and at very least they must have felt that those examples proved that a collected edition could find a publisher and a market. They may very well have circulated a proposal for their volume to various stationers before entering into the eventual arrangements with William and Isaac Jaggard.[9]

William Jaggard, as many have noted, already had experience printing Shakespeare, though not necessarily of a sort that would have automatically suggested him to the actors for their memorial project. First, in 1599 Jaggard printed *The Passionate Pilgrim* with a title page proclaiming it as "By W. Shakespeare," though in fact the work is properly an anthology containing only four sonnets by Shakespeare, two of which are from *Love's Labor's Lost*. The majority of the book is verse by other contemporary poets, including Christopher Marlowe, Walter Raleigh, and Richard Barnfield. The title page attribution attracted no attention until 1612, when the third edition appeared, this time significantly expanded by including pieces by Thomas Heywood, the rights to which Jaggard controlled. The 1612 edition advertises the additional material, but Shakespeare's name remains the only one on the title page (Fig. 14). Not surprisingly, Heywood objected. In an epistle added to his *An Apology for Actors* (1612), he protested "the manifest iniury done" him by Jaggard's cavalier decision to include his poems in a volume issued under Shakespeare's name, fearing that it would inevitably "put the world in opinion I might steale them from him and hee, to do himselfe right hath since published them in his own name." Heywood added that Shakespeare too was "much offended with M. Jaggard (that he altogether unknowne to him) presumed to make so bold with his name" (sig. G4^r). Other than Heywood's

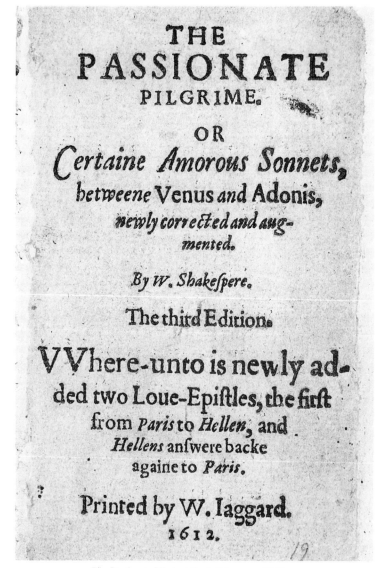

14. *The Passionate Pilgrim* (1612), title page, STC 22343

comment, we know nothing of Shakespeare's response to the episode, but Jaggard did cancel the title page of the unsold copies and reprint *The Passionate Pilgrim* without the assertion of Shakespeare's authorship (Fig. 15).

This was not the last irregularity that marked Jaggard's relationship with Shakespeare's work. Notoriously, in 1619, Jaggard and Thomas Pavier had joined together to publish a collection of ten of Shakespeare's plays (in point of fact only eight were by Shakespeare; the other two, *A Yorkshire Tragedy* and *1 Sir John Oldcastle*, were plays that had been falsely attributed to him). The project may well have derailed when the King's men successfully implored the Lord Chamberlain to order that "no playes that his Ma^tyes players so play shalbe printed w^thout consent of som[m]e of them."[10] And that consent was not forthcoming. Most scholars have argued that the intervention from on high stopped the planned-for collection, but, as printing had already started, Pavier and Jaggard decided to go forward, discontinuing, however, the sequential pagination that had been begun and issuing the plays individually, some with falsely dated title pages (Fig. 16), presumably so they would seem old stock that could be safely sold at Pavier's shop in Ivy Lane.[11]

Why then would Heminge and Condell turn to Jaggard's firm to print the volume they envisaged? Various answers have been proposed, but in truth the problem may not demand as much ingenuity as has been spent on it. First of all, Jaggard's behavior in both cases was not some unheard of outrage but the kind of irregular, opportunistic practice that most stationers had on occasion engaged in. Swinburne called Jaggard an "infamous pirate, liar and thief,"[12] but he was in fact a successful and respected member of the Stationers' Company, and if from time to time he operated at the edge of propriety and legality, he was in this regard little different from most of his fellows who, given the insecurity of the book trade, had learned to be opportunistic and pragmatic; and if at times he crossed over that edge, he could be – and obviously was – readily forgiven.

But the real answer is probably simpler still; Heminge and Condell contracted with the Jaggards to print the folio because the Jaggards were willing to do it. Few stationers would have been

THE
PASSIONATE
PILGRIME.

OR

Certaine Amorous Sonnets,
betweene *Venus* and *Adonis,*
newly corrected and aug-
mented.

The third Edition.

Where-unto is newly ad-
ded two *Loue-Epistles, the first*
from *Paris* to *Hellen,* and
Hellens *answere backe*
againe to *Paris.*

Printed by W. Iaggard.
1612.

15. *The Passionate Pilgrim* (1612), title page cancel, STC 22343

THE
Chronicle Hiſtory
of Henry the fift, with his
battell fought at *Agin Court* in
France. Together with an-
cient Piſtoll.

As it hath bene ſundry times playd by the Right Honou-
rable the Lord Chamberlaine his
Seruants.

Printed for *T. P.* 1608.

16. *Henry V* 1619 Pavier quarto title page (falsely dated 1608)

eager or even able to undertake a project the size of the Shakespeare folio. The commitment of resources and the impossibility of any quick profits would make it an unattractive venture for any but the most ambitious publishers. But the Jaggards apparently were willing to take it on.[13] In 1622, the first notice of the folio appears in a catalogue of English books that was printed for circulation at the biannual Frankfurt book fair: "Playes, written by M. William Shakespeare, all in one volume, printed by Isaak Iaggard, in fol."[14]

Clearly the Jaggards had anticipated that printing would be completed before it actually was, but as revealing is the fact that the book is said to be "printed by Isaak Iaggard." What is surprising here is not that it is Isaac who is named; he was William's oldest son, who had gradually assumed more day-to-day responsibility for the shop as his father's blindness limited his own involvements. What is surprising is that the book is announced as Jaggard's at all. The catalogue's phrase, "Printed by," means what we mean today by "published by." The printer, to be precise, was the person who manufactured the book in his shop, the owner of both the press and type; the publisher was the person who acquired the copy, paid for its printing, and was the wholesale distributor of the printed books. In practice, stationers, the comprehensive term for the diverse activities of the book trade, usually worked in various capacities, sometimes functioning solely as a book's printer, sometimes as its publisher, and sometimes only as a bookseller of other publisher's products, or in some cases combining two or all three of these roles.[15]

The Jaggards had increasingly defined their business primarily as a printing firm. Nonetheless, the Frankfurt catalogue's announcement of the forthcoming folio as a Jaggard book means that in this case they worked not only as printers but also as publishers of the volume. And when the folio did finally reach print, somewhat later than the optimistic catalogue projection, its colophon says the volume was "Printed at the Charges of W. Jaggard, Ed. Blount, I. Smithweeke, and W. Aspley." The Jaggards had obviously assembled a consortium of stationers to make the costly publication a reality. William Jaggard, in fact, was dead by the time the folio appeared, having died in early November of 1623, probably within weeks of the folio's completion; the colophon, however, printed earlier with the completion of *Cymbeline*, could not have anticipated his death. John Smethwick and William Aspley were mainly booksellers, and were, no doubt, invited into the syndicate rather late in the game, when it was discovered that between them they controlled the rights to six of Shakespeare's plays, which they probably allowed to be published in exchange for a percentage of the venture.

Edward Blount is a more interesting figure.[16] He had worked with William Jaggard on Edward Dering's *Workes* (1614), but how early he became involved in the Shakespeare folio is unclear. When the biannual catalogue of English books available at Frankfurt was issued in April of 1624, the spring following the folio's publication, an entry reads: "Master William Shakesperes workes, printed for Edward Blount, in fol."[17] Possibly Blount was involved with the Jaggards as the project initially took shape, as a number of scholars have argued,[18] though his absence from the 1622 catalogue entry and presence in the 1624 inventory suggests that, more likely, he became involved with them sometime after the bookfair in 1622, perhaps invited into partnership once the dismaying dimensions of the undertaking had become clear. If Blount were indeed the volume's "principal venturer," as R. Crompton Rhodes claims (*Shakespeare's First Folio*, p. 12), it seems improbable that the 1622 Frankfurt catalogue would not register his activity. Neither of the Jaggards was particularly self-promoting, and there seems little reason to disguise the truth. The evidence of the *Catalogue of such English Bookes, as lately haue bene, and now are in Printing for Publication* (1618), which William Jaggard prepared and printed, is that Jaggard was remarkably scrupulous in his ascriptions of books to their publishers. Blount's absence from the 1622 Frankfurt catalogue, then, seemingly demands to be understood in the simplest fashion, strongly arguing for his absence from the project itself until it was well under way.

Yet whenever Blount was invited to join the consortium, the invitation was a felicitous one. Blount was not just another investor to share the risk, but a publisher particularly likely to be attracted to a literary project, and one whose presence might even lend it some prestige. He had apprenticed with William Ponsonby, the man

R. B. McKerrow calls "the most important publisher of the Elizabethan period,"[19] during the period when Ponsonby published, among other things, Sidney's *Arcadia* and Spenser's *Faerie Queene*. And Blount's publications reveal his own uncommon literary sophistication. He published Marlowe's *Hero and Leander*, and in the dedication Blount identifies himself as a friend "to the unhappily desceased author of this poem." His dramatic publications reveal an atypical sense of the drama as an emergent literary form. He published the first collection of plays written in English – a quarto edition of two of William Alexander's closet dramas, published as *The Monarchick Tragedies* in 1604 and an augmented edition of four plays published three years later – and Blount also was responsible for the first play collection published after the appearance of the Shakespeare folio. In 1632 he published a duodecimo edition of *Sixe Court Comedies* by John Lyly, recognizing these then fifty-year-old plays specifically as literary delights: "*Thou canst not repent the Reading ouer them: when Old* Iohn Lilly *is merry with thee in thy Chamber, Thou shalt say Few (or None) of our Poets now are such witty Companions*" (sig. [A]3^v-4^r). In 1603, and again in 1613, he published John Florio's translation of Montaigne's *Essays*; and in 1612, he published the first part of Thomas Shelton's translation of Cervantes's *Don Quixote* and eight years later the second part (and that within three weeks of its first publication in Madrid). As the publisher of play collections by Cartwright, Shakespeare, and Lyly, he might be said, if not actually to have established the drama as a literary genre, at least to have been among the very first to recognize its potential to become one. And perhaps more consequentially, as the English publisher of Marlowe, Montaigne, Cervantes, and Shakespeare, Blount might be said to have invented, if not precisely the Renaissance for England, at least its first Great Books course.

If, however, Blount's involvement helped bring about the success of the Shakespeare folio, the folio seemingly did little to assure Blount's. In the years immediately following its publication, he slowly began to withdraw from the book trade, publishing nothing in the five years following the folio's publication and, in all, only eight more books before his death in 1632. Unsurprisingly, he added no apprentices to his business after 1623.[20] In 1624, he sold his interest in the extraordinarily popular *Hero and Leander*,[21] and the following year, he was forced to assign his portion of the profitable English Stock to George Swinhowe in partial fulfillment of an unpaid debt of £160.[22] In 1627, he sold his bookshop to Robert Allott, and, three years later, sold Allott his share in Shakespeare's plays.[23]

Blount's diminished activity must be attributed to some combination of advancing age and decreasing fortunes, but probably should not be traced directly to his involvement with the folio. While neither his investment nor that of any of his partners would have been recoverable in the first year or two following publication, the volume did turn a remarkably quick profit and justified a second edition only nine years after the first. The Jonson folio, in contrast, took twenty-four years to warrant a second printing.[24]

Clearly the publication of the Shakespeare folio was a success, but one that, if passionately wished for, could not have been confidently predicted. A large, expensive volume of plays was not guaranteed to sell well, and whatever profits might eventually come were certain to be delayed for many months after the initial investment. Even the small, inexpensive quartos, as we have seen, were a risky proposition for a publisher to take on, dependent largely on enthusiastic playgoers or disappointed would-be ones. The folio, however, anticipated and demanded dedicated (and reasonably well-to-do) play *readers*, without being certain they existed in any great number. Jonson, of course, was chided for his audacity in turning culturally demotic plays into an elite literary genre. "Pray tell me *Ben*, where doth the mystery lurke, / What others call a play you call a worke," as an often-quoted contemporary wrote; and Henry Fitzgeffrey, the year after the Jonson folio's publication, found the author's ambitions characteristic of the age, mocking the presumption of "Bookes *made of* Ballads: Workes: of Plays."[25]

But the Shakespeare folio, if it avoids the aggressive classicizing gestures of the Jonson folio, is in a sense an even more presumptuous undertaking. Jonson's folio included nine plays, but what is often ignored is that the plays were but a part of Jonson's *Workes*, which also included 133 numbered epigrams, the various poems of "The Forrest," and the masques and other entertainments. The Shakespeare folio was the first to insist that a man might be an "author" on the basis of his plays alone, and, more remarkably, on the basis of plays written exclusively for the professional stage. And where the Jonson folio is clearly selective about the inclusion of plays (Jonson admitted to Drummond that "the half of his comedies were not in print"[26]), the Shakespeare folio insists that the volume sets forth "all his Comedies, histories, and Tragedies." Indeed the continuing efforts to secure the rights to *Troilus and Cressida* and finally get it into the volume (a process that, as Peter Blayney has shown, resulted in three separate states of the folio[27]) alone must demonstrate how strong the determination was for an inclusive collection. The volume is, then, unique not only because it is the first folio volume completely made up of English plays, but also because it is the first collection in any format that was designed as the *complete* plays of its author.

In fact, as we know, at least three plays that Shakespeare had at least a hand in are missing: *Pericles*, *The Two Noble Kinsmen*, and *Sir Thomas More*. But arguably their absence confirms the radical design of the volume. *The Two Noble Kinsmen* is unquestionably a collaboration with John Fletcher, first published in 1634 as by "Mr. John Fletcher and Mr. William Shakespeare," their names yoked together in brackets on the quarto title page. The book of *Sir Thomas More* is a manuscript of a play written about 1592 and subsequently revised, at least in part in response to its censoring by the Master of the Revels, Edward Tilney, and whatever role Shakespeare had in it, usually assumed to be only the 146 lines in the handwriting known as "Hand D," it too is unquestionably collaborative.[28]

Pericles is a more problematic case. Published first in quarto in 1609, it is attributed on its title page to Shakespeare, but it is not included in the 1623 folio, appearing first in a collected edition only with the reissue of the third folio in 1664, as one of seven plays added in a supplement. The seven had all appeared in early quartos with Shakespeare's name or initials, but *Pericles* is the only one plausibly thought to be his. Even bibliographically a distinction is visible. *Pericles* appears first with its own separate pagination (1–20) and signatures; the other six were clearly added after, paginated together (1–100) and with continuous signatures. The odd physical structure of the supplement is the only sign of whatever obscure distinction its publisher, Philip Chetwind, intended.

Nonetheless, modern bibliography has accepted it, and *Pericles* now generally appears unquestioned in the canon of Shakespeare's plays. One exception is the recent, complete Oxford edition, edited by Stanley Wells and Gary Taylor. The Oxford editors include it, but argue that the play is a collaboration, insisting that at least the first nine scenes are by George Wilkins. This is not the occasion to examine that evidence, or their claim that Wilkins's prose novella, *The Painful Adventures of Pericles, Prince of Tyre*, should be considered "a 'reported text' of the play,"[29] or the aggressive editorial procedures based on those commitments that produce the Oxford version.

Whatever my reservations about the Oxford text and the assumptions underlying it, I do, however, wonder if indeed the play is not a collaboration, or, at very least, if its absence from the first folio does not reflect a belief that it was. No one has offered a very compelling explanation for the play's omission. It had been published as by Shakespeare, and had been successful both on stage (Jonson complaining, as late as 1629, of the continued popularity of such a "mouldy tale"), and in the bookstalls (six editions appearing between 1609 and 1635, thus marking it as among the most popular of Shakespeare's plays in print).

The issue seems not to be one of rights, because, while the play is indeed one of those entered to a publisher and hence belonging to him for print purposes, that publisher was Blount himself, who had entered the play on 20 May 1608. It is possible that Blount had forgotten his entry; on that same day he had also entered *Antony and Cleopatra*, and he seems to have overlooked his title to that play, for he re-enters it along with fifteen others, just days before the folio was to be published in 1623, to confirm the publishers' right to publish the plays they had received from the King's men.

But even if there was forgetfulness on the part of Blount, it will not quite do as an explanation for the absence of *Pericles* from the folio, since the other major figure in the volume's publication, Jaggard, had printed the play in 1619, as part of the collection that he and Pavier attempted. And that same year, the King's men performed the play at court. Clearly, whatever caused the play's omission from the first folio, it cannot be mere oversight. Indeed as all of the volume's principals were somehow involved in the play, it is hard to believe its absence from the folio was not deliberate.

It is not inconceivable, of course, that Blount had sold his title, though no record of any transfer exists. *The Late, and much admired Play, Called Pericles, Prince of Tyre* was published twice by Henry Gosson in 1609, again in 1611, possibly by Simon Stafford (though it seems more likely that Stafford merely printed the play, as he did with each of the eleven other dramatic publications with which he was involved), and then once more in 1619 by Pavier, all without any further entry in the Register; but many transactions between stationers must have taken place that remained unrecorded. Pavier's 1619 publication was, of course, the most recent printing, and he may well have purchased the title to the play from Gosson (or Stafford). At very least, Pavier's apparent title should have made the play available to the syndicate, as he seemingly leased the other titles in his possession to them. If his title was thought to be somehow faulty (though his widow seems successfully to have transferred it on 4 August 1626, along with other of "Shakesperes plaies," to Edward Brewster and Robert Bird, who print the play as "by Will. Shakespeare" in 1630), Blount and Jaggard might well then have risked the play's publication on the basis of Blount's 1608 entry. In any case, it is difficult to see why Blount and Jaggard would not have pursued the rights to *Pericles* if they thought it Shakespeare's, as they did with the other plays belonging to publishers outside their syndicate, or would not have felt free to publish it as their own.

Given what is certainly known of the various involvements of all the folio's principals with the play, it is hard to resist the conclusion that *Pericles* was purposefully excluded from the volume – and on the same grounds that both *The Two Noble Kinsmen* and *Sir Thomas More* were omitted: Shakespeare in all three plays was a collaborator rather than the primary author, and in that diminished role his accomplishment was felt not to require recognition – or indeed to permit it. The folio claims to present all the plays Shakespeare actually "wrote," not the ones to which he contributed. It reflects precisely the anxiety about authorship that Jonson displays in unashamedly erasing the contribution of a second hand that allowed *Sejanus* to be performed as he claims the play as his own. If Jonson creates himself as an author in part by denying his collaborations, Shakespeare is created as an author in part by having them denied for him.

This, of course, raises the issue of *Henry VIII*, which most recent scholarship assumes is a collaboration by Shakespeare and Fletcher, although it appears in the folio as the last of ten histories. Here, then, is an apparent exception to the principle I have just formulated. A play that seemingly was collaborative does appear in the folio as Shakespeare's own. Now it is possible that recent attribution studies have it wrong. No contemporary evidence exists to identify *Henry VIII* as a collaboration, and indeed it was not until 1850 that the claim for a second hand was first urged.[30] Perhaps the play's very presence in the folio could then be held to argue single authorship, although the manifest circularity of this reasoning makes for an unsatisfying argument.

Scholars applying sophisticated statistical tests measuring stylistic and linguistic habits seem persuaded that two hands are responsible for the play, and they confidently differentiate the "Shakespeare" scenes from the "Fletcher" scenes.[31] I do not wish to challenge the consensus insisting on Fletcher's contribution to *Henry VIII*, lacking both the linguistic and the statistical skills even to assess the methodologies used in making the case; but it is worth observing that the folio text on which all analysis must be based is heavily mediated and in ways still not fully understood. Not only are compositorial syntactic and spelling habits inevitably reflected in the printed text, but also the underlying manuscript is as likely to be scribal as authorial, thus potentially introducing yet another set of non-authorial linguistic habits into the sample on which the attribution studies are based.

What is certain, however, is that Heminge and Condell, who presumably would have been aware of any collaboration, present the play as Shakespeare's own. At exactly the time when Beaumont and Fletcher, working together as collaborators – "one poet in a paire of friends," as one of the commendatory poems in their 1647 folio has it (sig. D1ᵛ) – had supplanted Shakespeare as the primary source of plays for the King's men, the two oldest (and still active) members of the company in their role as Shakespeare's first editors give Shakespeare sole credit for what most scholars believe is an example of his collaboration with another playwright.

It would seem that, from the point of view of the company, acknowledging Fletcher's share would be good business – the folio serving to advertise the continuity of their present playwrights with the company's past greatness that the folio itself is in part designed to celebrate – but it is impossible to know why the two editors did not do so. Perhaps it is indeed that the disintegrationists since Spedding have been wrong: that the play is Shakespeare's alone; or perhaps Heminge and Condell had merely forgotten that Fletcher had a share in the play when they collected the manuscript from the theatre about a decade after the play was written and brought it to Jaggard's shop; or perhaps the nature of Fletcher's participation was such that it did not disrupt their sense of Shakespeare's primary responsibility for the play, as Middleton's hand in *Macbeth* does not generally trouble our sense of it as a play by Shakespeare.[32]

I am tempted mainly by this last explanation. Collaboration is an inescapable fact of play production, not merely in the obvious sense that actors and other theatre practitioners impose their understandings upon the authorial script, but also because the script itself is regularly revised, cut, and structured for every new production and venue. If Shakespeare himself would have most likely revised his own plays during his tenure with the company, with his retirement, and certainly with his death in 1616, other hands, not improbably including Fletcher's, would have reshaped his plays with no necessary deference to Shakespeare's original design (as the plays' history on the Restoration stage makes clear).[33] And, of course, at the very moment at which the folio was being produced, most of the new plays being performed by the King's men were collaborative from their very moment of origin. Collaboration cannot, then, have been for Heminge and Condell something that would ordinarily stigmatize a play text.

Nonetheless, the Shakespeare folio is obviously designed to establish Shakespeare as a single (and singular) author rather than a playwright working collaboratively within the economies of the theatre. As the volume does not obviously require *Henry VIII*, Heminge and Condell's decision to include the play seems to me, therefore, to point inevitably to their belief that it satisfied the conditions of single authorship; that is, that it could reasonably be said to be "by William Shakespeare" within the usual conditions of play production. If most readers were not then in a position to know better and possibly object, certainly their fellow theatre practitioners – and not least John Fletcher – would know if this claim was untrue; and, if they were in no position to do anything about it, they would awkwardly be around to remind the two aging actors of any presumption in claiming the play for Shakespeare. But Heminge and Condell seemingly feel no anxiety about the inclusion, and they confidently present the play, exactly as they present the thirty-five other plays with which it shares the volume, as Shakespeare's own (if not precisely, as none could be, his alone).[34]

As a number of recent scholars have argued, the ambition of the folio is to create Shakespeare as an author, a project once thought to be the design only of eighteenth-century scholars like Capell and Malone. If indeed this is the intention of the 1623 folio, the exclusion of what were recognized as collaborative plays (and a generous understanding of what was understood as authorial) might easily be thought by the volume's principal architects appropriate, arguably even necessary. The published volume presents itself radically as Shakespeare's work. "Mr. William / SHAKE-SPEARES / COMEDIES, / HISTORIES, & / TRAGEDIES. / Published according to the True Originall Copies" proclaims the title page (Fig. 17), and it offers a stark, engraved portrait by Martin Droeshout as witness to its authenticity. Hooded eyes engage us from a large head floating oddly above the unfashionable ruff. The short poem on the facing page, however, asks us to look away, contesting the engraver's power to arrest us with Shakespeare's image. "O, could he but haue drawne his wit / As well in brasse, as he hath hit / His face, the print would then surpasse / All, that was euer writ in Brasse. / But, since he cannot, Reader, looke / Not on his Picture, but his Booke." It is the book we should look to, the book where we are told we will discover not only what is authentically Shakespeare's but indeed what is authentically Shakespeare.[35]

But what is in that book? Shakespeare is, of course, there somewhere, but certainly not whole and unadulterated; the texts themselves are based on scribal copies and authorial manuscripts, annotated quartos and prompt books; they reflect both first thoughts and later theatrical additions. They reveal his active engagement in the collaborations of the theater company and his passive acceptance of the collaborations in the printing house. The volume, however, would tell a different story. Shakespeare is no

Mr. WILLIAM

SHAKESPEARES

COMEDIES,
HISTORIES, &
TRAGEDIES.

Publiſhed according to the True Originall Copies.

Martin Droeshout sculpsit London.

L O N D O N
Printed by Iſaac Iaggard, and Ed. Blount. 1623.

17. 1623 Shakespeare folio title page, STC 22273.

longer a collaborator in any sense but, as Ben Jonson's commendatory poem names him, "The AVTHOR Mr. William Shakespeare," sole creator of the plays within. The theatrical authorizations that mark the quartos are gone; there is no mention that any text is here "as it was played"; indeed the acting companies are never mentioned by name. The names of the principal players are printed, though interestingly enough on a page that is part of an afterthought to the preliminaries and indeed one which is headed "The Workes of William Shakespeare." The texts themselves are offered as new and improved, or, more precisely, as original and still uncontaminated, the title page promising that the plays are "Truly set forth according to their first ORIGINALL."

With that claim, the volume pursues its objective, of creating Shakespeare as the author he never was or wanted to be. Heminge and Condell knew better than any how his first originals were modified in the theater (and no doubt often for the better): altered to clarify relationships, cut to improve pacing, adjusted to allow time for costume changes, adapted to fit the staging requirements of different playing spaces, revised when a joke grew old or situation tired or when some contemporary event might provide an opportunity to make an old play newly relevant. It was precisely to avoid the uncontrollable compromises performance demands that Jonson, as is well known, turned to print, self-consciously reconstructing his plays as literature. His decision to publish his plays in carefully supervised print versions that aggressively deny their origin seems almost inevitable given his ambivalence about the theater, evident in his periodic vows to "leave the loathed stage."[36] But that Heminge and Condell, both of whom had spent their lives happily working in the theater and who knew Shakespeare primarily from the theater, would so readily disregard the theater in the commemorative volume is much more surprising.

One might think that they would emphasize the fruitful collaborations of playwright and actor, the popularity of the plays among audiences of all ages and social classes, or even suggest, as some play texts did, that the true life of drama is on the stage. But they make only a single gesture to the theatrical auspices of what is published. In their dedication to the Herberts they comment that so great was their Lordships' "likings of the seuerall parts, when

they were acted" that even before it was published "the Volume
ask'd to be yours." But rather than suggest the aesthetic priority of
the staged play, here its priority is merely temporal; and indeed the
play as performed is imagined not as the essential experience that
the published play can only and belatedly approximate but as a
more ephemeral form of the volume itself – the volume *in potentia*
– now at last fully realized and able to be claimed.

If Heminge and Condell unexpectedly slight the theater, the
reasons are not hard to guess. The volume is aimed at readers or,
more exactly, at buyers, who may very well be put off by a more
overt theatrical claim. Plays were still subliterary, and play quartos,
as we have seen, cheap pamphlets, often denigrated as riff-raff and
pointedly excluded, as has often been noted, from the books the
Bodleian would collect. Even the Jonson folio did not make its way
into the collection by the time of the 1620 catalogue, but, as is well
known, early in 1624, the library received a copy of the Shakespeare
folio, had it expensively bound, and added it to the collection.

The Bodleian copy was donated as the result of an agreement
made in 1610 for the library to receive "one perfect Booke" printed
by any member of the Stationers' Company,[37] but individuals
would have had to buy the folio for about £1, somewhat less if purchased unbound. Sir Edward Dering's account books on 5
December 1623 record the purchase of "2 volumes of Shakespear's
playes" for £2 (and one of Jonson's, for which he paid 9 shillings).[38]
At a pound, the book was expensive and its market obviously more
limited than that for the six-penny play quartos. Though there are
some examples of collectors of playbooks in all formats, the buyers
of the folio were probably on balance different from those that
bought quartos, both wealthier and more desirous of having their
literary tastes flattered by the book they would buy.

Thus the book presents itself as literary. The texts that have been
"collected & publish'd" are said to be set forth exactly as they
flowed from their author's imaginings, uncontaminated by the contingencies of the printing shop or of the playhouse. It is the ideal
text of editorial desire, or so it claims: a collection of plays
"Published according to the True Originall Copies." It cannot, of
course, be so. Heminge and Condell must certainly have known
that of the manuscripts they provided the printer at most three

were Shakespeare's autograph papers. The others were either scribal transcripts or the bookkeepers' marked playbooks, though the distinction would not have been of any interest to them. Scribal versions tend to rationalize texts, cleaning up inconsistencies, regularizing speech headings, spelling, punctuation, even, at times, metrics; theatrical copies would inevitably have recorded interpolations and cuts made to enable the scripts to play. In either case, the author's "true original" has long been lost. And even that "true original" would bear an uncertain relation to Shakespeare's final intentions. Yet Heminge and Condell insist that "Where before" readers of Shakespeare's plays "were abus'd with diuerse stolne, and surreptitious copies, maimed, and deformed by the frauds and stealthes of iniurious imposters that expos'd them: euen those, are now offer'd to your view cur'd, and perfect of their limbes; and all the rest, absolute in their numbers, as he conceiu'd the[m]."[39]

Scholars have, understandably, aggressively mined this remarkable sentence for evidence about the earliest transmission of Shakespeare's plays, and have constructed influential narratives based upon Heminge and Condell's distinction between the "diuerse stolen, and surreptitious copies" that were "maimed and deformed" and "all the rest." The consensus shaped by the groundbreaking work of the new bibliographers (i.e., the not-so-new bibliographic scholars active mainly in the first third of the twentieth century, A. W. Pollard, W. W. Greg, and R. B. McKerrow) has it that the first set of terms does not apply to all the pre-folio quartos but only "to plays of which the Quartos have bad texts and the Folio good ones."[40] This now common understanding has it that Heminge and Condell differentiate those quarto texts (like Q1 *Hamlet* or Q1 *Romeo*) that seemingly derive not from Shakespeare's manuscripts but from unauthorized transcripts of the play made by a reporter or one or more actors (hence "maimed and deformed") and that were published without the authority of the acting company (hence "stolne and surreptitious") from "the rest" of the plays in the folio, a group that in turn encompasses two further categories of texts: the "good" quartos, i.e., those editions printed from legally acquired copy that was either Shakespeare's own manuscript or a transcript of it, and the playhouse manuscripts of the previously unpublished plays.

Though the distinctions are elegant and underpin a number of the most influential ideas of the new bibliography, they seem to me unlikely. First of all, they depend upon an extremely strained reading of the sentence, insisting upon three categories of texts where Heminge and Condell offer only two: the previously "deformed" texts that are now offered "cur'd" of their defects and "all the rest" that are still exactly as Shakespeare "conceiu'd" them. And, second, the distinctions project an implausible and anachronistic sense of bibliographic sophistication upon the two actors. An author might well complain – and indeed some did (though interestingly never Shakespeare) – about an unauthorized printing, but an actor would be unlikely to notice or to care, having always worked in contexts where theatrical requirements took precedence over the integrity of authorial design and where the publication of plays was generally an irrelevance, if not an inconvenience. Even in those cases where the King's men had actively opposed the publication of their plays the quality of the available texts was not the concern.

Perhaps if it could be proven that the texts for the "good" quartos were indeed purchased directly from the company, while those for the "bad" quartos were pirated editions, then there would at least be a profit motive that would explain the sensitivity; but the familiar bibliographic distinction owes far more to scholarly desire than to the facts of the case.[41] There is little basis for assuming that a "bad" text was inevitably irregularly published or that a "good" one reached print only with the acting company's consent.

I take it, rather, that Heminge and Condell distinguish only two kinds of texts: one, the "stolne and surreptitious copies," simply consists of the group of plays that has already been set out in print, "good" and "bad" quartos together; and the other, "all the rest," is comprised of the previously unpublished playscripts to this point safely held in the hands of the actors. In the folio Heminge and Condell bring both groups together: those vagrant play texts, previously "maimed and deformed" in the process of their publication, now "cur'd" (through some unspecified editorial labor); and Shakespeare's manuscripts, which, having been continuously sheltered from the depredations of the publishing process, already perfectly reveal Shakespeare's intentions, and so can be printed exactly "as he conceiued the[m]."

What prevents this straightforward explanation of Heminge and Condell's sentence from being readily accepted is that scholars quite correctly have observed that although some of the early quartos can be thought "surreptitious" and "deformed," others clearly cannot, and these in many cases had served as the copy for the folio texts. If Heminge and Condell are accurately describing the nature of the early texts, their claim about the "diuerse" editions that had previously circulated obviously cannot, then, refer to all of the earlier printings, and, so scholars, in their desire to affirm both the integrity of the folio editors and the texts they set forth, wrench the sentence to make it mean what their understanding of the bibliographic facts demands.

But the very insistence that the prefatory letter provides an exact description of the characteristics of the early texts works to undercut the interpretation of the two editors' claim. At most two of the plays appearing in the folio might be thought to satisfy the definition of a text now "perfected" and published regularly that before existed only in a version that was both "surreptitious" and "maimed." The "bad" quartos of *Loves Labor's Lost* (if there was indeed an earlier, defective printing), *Romeo and Juliet*, and *Hamlet* had already been superseded by better texts and indeed ones that the folio versions of these plays in various ways depend upon. The early texts of *2 and 3 Henry VI*, both of which are generally considered somehow defective, were seemingly fully authorized publications, part two of *Henry VI* properly registered in 1594, the registration apparently also covering part three, as the rights to both parts were transferred to Thomas Pavier from Thomas Millington in 1602. *Richard III* (1597) and *King Lear* (1608) also were both properly registered, *Richard III* to Andrew Wise on 20 October 1597 and *Lear* to Nathaniel Butter and John Busby on 26 November 1607; and while both texts differ markedly from their folio versions, containing lines absent from the folio and missing lines there present, neither displays the kind of textual corruption usually thought to be characteristic of a "bad" quarto.

The quarto versions of *Henry V* and *Merry Wives*, however, may more plausibly be considered non-authorial texts (though Q1 *Henry V*, perhaps abridged for performance, is entirely coherent, its deficiencies largely a function of its inadequate stage directions; Q1

Merry Wives seems a better candidate to be a reported text), and in both cases some abnormality surrounds their publication. *Henry V* was published in 1600 by Thomas Millington and John Busby without registration and in the face of a "stay" against its printing recorded on 4 August 1600. *Merry Wives*, however, was registered; John Busby entered it on 18 January 1602, but its rights were immediately assigned to Arthur Johnson. The unusual practice has appeared to some as telling evidence of Busby's shrewd if not shifty effort to avoid liability for the purchase of unauthorized copy, although it seems far more likely to have been a perfectly legitimate method of generating a small profit with very little risk by selling the rights to a play rather than undertaking its publishing.[42]

In any case, if merely two of the thirty-six plays of the folio can be considered to have previously circulated only in editions both "surreptitious" and "maimed" (and even of these two, one is arguably not "surreptitious" and the other arguably not "maimed"), it hardly seems enough to bear the full weight of the radical differentiation of authorized (and "perfect") and unauthorized (and "deformed") texts upon which Heminge and Condell's sanction of the folio versions rests. Instead, I would argue that their contested sentence means exactly what it seems to say; the plays in print at the time of the publishing of the folio are what Heminge and Condell deride and what they distinguish from the putatively authentic texts that appear in their volume.

I am not, however, suggesting that we should, therefore, ignore the compelling research of Pollard, McKerrow, and Greg, and return to Malone's unduly pessimistic conclusion about the early quartos: that "undoubtedly they were *all* surreptitious, that is stolen from the playhouse, and printed without the consent of the author or the proprietors."[43] "Undoubtedly" the early printings were not all unauthorized or defective. What I am claiming is only that Heminge and Condell *say* they were, perhaps because to men of the theater a cheaply published playbook could be nothing else, but mainly, no doubt, to increase the appeal of the newly published folio volume. The two actors simply assert that "before" the folio was available readers were "abus'd" with corrupted texts and that "now" they may enjoy Shakespeare's plays "perfect of their limbes" and "absolute in their numbers, as he conceiu'd the[m]."

The sentence enacts the classic "before and after" advertiser's strategy, and can hardly be taken as a definitive account of the early texts. It is testimony to our desire for the authentic Shakespeare that it has ever been thought to be so. The plays in print prior to the folio are not as degraded as Heminge and Condell suggest, nor are the plays that had escaped print as unadulterated as they profess. But Heminge and Condell's bibliographic claim should never have been taken as an authoritative textual history. It is a motivated fantasy of textual production, and interestingly one exactly like the image of Shakespeare's process of creation: "His mind and hand went together: And what he thought, he vttered with that easinesse, that wee haue scarse receiued from him a blot in his papers."[44] Shakespeare seemingly writes without labor, and these published texts, unlike any previous ones, reproduce his effortless creation also without flaw or blemish. Writing and printing go together exactly as did his "mind and hand."

In their epistle, Heminge and Condell establish Shakespeare as an author by erasing the very conditions of his art, the active principles of its realization. The multiple agencies of the theater and the printing house, even the agency of Shakespeare's own work, are denied. The epistle insists that the plays are set forth exactly as the playwright "conceiu'd the[m]," but the processes of their materialization improbably leave no trace. In Heminge and Condell's account, Shakespeare's absolute authority is left uncontested and intact – or, more exactly, their account does not *leave* Shakespeare's authority unchallenged, it is the very means by which that authority is invented. Shakespeare never had it, and, unlike Jonson, he had never tried to claim it.

Arguably, today much more is at stake in the assertion of Shakespeare's unique authorship, for he has come to play another role he never sought, as the witness and guarantor of western moral and social values; for Heminge and Condell, and the publishing syndicate that put together the volume, it was perhaps much simpler. Heminge and Condell offer the book to its hoped-for readers and invite them to judge as they see fit: "Iudge your sixepen'orth, your shillings worth, your fiue shillings worth at a time or higher, so you rise to the iust rates, and welcome. But, what euer you do, Buy." "Read him," they urge; and "again and again"; but the bottom line, we might well say, for the publishers is: "What euer you do, Buy." Heminge and Condell may indeed have been, as they claimed, "without ambition" for "selfe-profit," but Jaggard, Blount, Smethwick and Aspley could not afford to have felt similarly.

The commercial context of the folio must not be forgotten. Today it seems obvious to us that the volume was the necessary and appropriate memorial to England's greatest playwright, but at the time all that was clear to Blount and his partners was that they had undertaken an expensive publishing project with no certainty of recovering their considerable investment.[45] If Shakespeare the writer must inevitably be found decentered and dispersed in the communities and collaborations of early modern play and book production, he has been purposefully and powerfully reconstituted as an "AVTHOR" in the commercial desires of the early modern book trade.[46]

Indeed, if Shakespeare cannot with any precision be called the creator of the book that bears his name, that book might be said to be the creator of Shakespeare. Ben Jonson, driven by a powerful literary ambition, actively sought his role as an author. Shakespeare, as we have seen, was largely indifferent to such individuation, comfortably working in the collaborative ethos of the theater.[47] But it is Shakespeare, of course, who has emerged as the towering figure of individual genius, never, however, having sought his greatness but having it thrust upon him seven years after he died.

CHAPTER THREE

From contemporary to classic; or, textual healing

I forget the name of the French author who says that the
English are Shakespeare mad. There are some grounds for
the assertion. We are Methodists in regard to Shakespeare.

John Boyle, earl of Orrery

The Shakespeare folio of 1623 was relatively quickly reprinted; a
mere nine years after it was published, a second edition appeared.
Testimony to the success of Heminge and Condell's memorial
project, the second folio (F2) was printed by Thomas Cotes for a
consortium of stationers, though only William Aspley and John
Smethwick still were alive from the group that had published the
first. Aspley and Smethwick retained their interest in the venture,
and joined with Cotes, Richard Hawkins, Richard Meighen, and
Robert Allott as publishers of the second. The volume's imprint
invariably names Cotes as the printer, but in its various states has
him printing "for" one or another of the other partners, suggesting that at least part of the arrangement between them was that
each would take a number of copies, presumably apportioned
according to their stake in the venture.

The new consortium again assembled rights to the plays, as the
copyrights achieved to publish the first folio apparently had
reverted to their owners.[1] On 19 July 1627, Dorothy Jaggard, Issac's
widow, had assigned "her parte in Shackspheere playes" to Cotes
and his brother Richard,[2] giving them a half interest in the sixteen
plays that had been registered by Blount and Jaggard on 8
November 1623. In 1630 Richard Cotes also acquired the rights to
Henry V, *Titus Andronicus*, and a play called *Yorke and Lancaster* (*2
Henry VI*, though possibly including *Part 3*) from Robert Bird, who,
four years earlier, had been assigned, along with Edward Brewster,

"M^r. Paviers right in Shakesperes plaies."[3] That same year, the Stationers' register records Blount's assignment of his rights in various copies, including the sixteen Shakespeare plays he had registered with Jaggard, to Robert Allott.[4] Between Allott and the Cotes brothers, then, rights to nineteen or, possibly, twenty plays had been achieved. Smethwick and Aspley still retained the six titles they had held between them when the first folio was published. In January 1630, Meighen had acquired the rights to *The Merry Wives of Windsor* from Arthur Johnson, and, two years earlier, Hawkins had received from Thomas Walkley the rights to "Orthello [*sic*] the more of Venice."[5]

The members of the consortium, then, between themselves controlled the rights to twenty-seven (or twenty-eight, if they owned both *2* and *3 Henry VI*) of the plays. The remaining titles were either assumed to be derelict or known to be held by other stationers, who presumably again leased their rights for the collected volume to the publishing syndicate. The volume itself is essentially a line-by-line reprint of the first folio, though the second edition does in places "correct" the text of the first. There is, however, nothing to suggest that any new material was consulted that would make these changes authoritative. On the other hand, Malone's judgment that "no one who wishes to peruse the plays of Shakespeare should even open the Second folio" is unnecessarily harsh (and indeed George Steevens in 1793 took some obvious pleasure in pointing out that Malone himself had obviously opened it, as his edition of 1790 adopted 186 corrections that first appeared in F2).[6]

Considerable editorial work on F2 was done from pages of the first folio, almost certainly in the printing house itself. Matthew Black and Matthias Shaaber count almost 1,700 changes from the 1623 folio, 623 of which have been regularly accepted in modern editions.[7] In large part what was done, beyond the correction of obvious typographical errors, was a form of modernization not much different from that which twentieth-century editors have characteristically undertaken with the text. Spelling and grammar are brought into accord, if somewhat less than systematically, with the changed linguistic environment of the early 1630s. The old ordinals "Fift" and "Sixt," for example, are changed to "Fifth" and "Sixth" in the running titles of the relevant *Henry* plays. "Who" and "whom" are usually regularized according to the more rigorous (i.e. latinate) grammatical assumptions of the seventeenth century (for example, at 2.2.6 in *The Winter's Tale*, where the first folio's "And one, who much I honour" is "corrected" to "And one, whom . . ."). "To" is generally differentiated from "too," "lose" from "loose," and about one quarter of the some 250 places in the first folio where a plural subject is followed by a singular verb are changed, so verb and subject now agree as modern grammar demands.

Efforts were made to rectify words or phrases in the first folio that were apparently corrupt. At least one of the correctors involved in preparing the text had useful classical training. He emended the flawed Latin of *Love's Labor's Lost* 4.2.91 (TLN 1257), which in the first folio reads "*Facile precor gellida, quando pecas omnia . . .,*" to the correct "*Fauste precor, gelida quando pecus omne . . .,*" no doubt recognizing the quotation from "good old" Mantuan's first eclogue (without, of course, inquiring whether the error was in fact dramatically desirable). He corrects the number of the Latin verbs that mark exits, so that *exeunt* more predictably appears where more than one person leaves the stage. He produces the proper form, "Anthropophagi," out of the first folio's "Antropophague" for the cannibals that Othello speaks of in his wondrous tale to Desdemona at 1.3.144; he recovers "Pantheon" from the "Parthan" of the first folio text of *Titus Andronicus* at 1.1.242; he recognizes the correct reading "Actium" in the first folio's "Action" in *Antony and Cleopatra* at 3.7.51; and he restores the proper spelling of the name of the famous Roman actor, Roscius, misrepresented by the first folio's "Rossius," in *Hamlet* (2.2.387).

Similarly, English words are replaced with others that seem to yield better sense, though again without any indication that the emendations were suggested by anything more than a thoughtful reading of the text. Hal's "unsavoury smiles" in *1 Henry IV* (1.2.76), which in the first folio designate the prince's various characterizations of Falstaff's melancholy, are correctly recognized in F2 as the Prince's "unsavoury similes"; similarly, the "miseries of Hecate" at 1.1.109 in the first folio text of *King Lear* become, more intelligibly, Hecate's "mysteries." In other places, however, the same procedures fail. In the first folio text of *Macbeth*, at 3.4.13, Macbeth's decision to seek out "the weyard Sisters" plausibly demands, by its unfamilar orthography, some editorial response; but rather than modernizing "weyard" as "weird," as most modern editions have done, or even as "wayward," F2 offers its readers an anxious Macbeth going forth in search of "the wizard Sisters."

In general what can be said about the second folio is that it shows a fundamental alertness to the disruptions in the first folio text, and that its efforts to fix these are logical rather than scholarly. The correctors seemingly had no access to early quartos or to any manuscripts of the plays. What the first Cambridge editors said in 1863 is accurate, if a bit ungenerous: "The emendations are evidently conjectural, and though occasionally right, appear more frequently to be wrong. They deserve no more respect than those of other guessers, except such as is due to their author's familiar acquaintance with the language and customs of Shakespeare's day, and possible knowledge of the acted plays."[8] The second folio, then, is not a work of any textual authority, though, as the Cambridge editors note, its temporal proximity to Shakespeare may well have given its correctors advantages that more rigorously scholarly editors necessarily have been denied.

If the second folio is, then, of little bibliographic value, it is still of unmistakable cultural significance. It not only works to confirm and consolidate the literary status of Shakespeare's plays that had been asserted by the first folio, but arguably it also marks the true beginning of the process that has driven virtually every subsequent venture of publishing Shakespeare's plays: the second folio initiates the procedures by which Shakespeare becomes the contemporary of his readers. By submitting his work to a process of modernization that can be more easily seen than heard – in the spelling of words, the normalizing of grammar, the standardization of capitalization and the use of italics, the regularizing of character's names, and so forth – Shakespeare's plays on the printed page, or, more precisely, *through* the printed page, escape their moment of creation and appear as contemporaneous with their moment of reception. Certainly some modernization was done in the first folio, but in the second folio the very principle of the text's preparation was to produce a volume that minimized, if not fully erased, the linguistic distance that had opened up between Shakespeare's writing and his seventeenth-century readers.

Nonetheless, if the volume self-consciously attempts to make Shakespeare the contemporary of his readers, the process did not obviously add to the edition's popularity. More than thirty years would pass before the collected plays would be published again. Although A. W. Pollard attributes the long hiatus between the second and third folios to the fact that "after 1639 political troubles spoilt the market for plays,"[9] some other explanation must be sought. Though the publication of plays did fall off during the war years, in the 1650s dramatic publication surged. Indeed, that period saw the third largest number of plays printed of any decade between 1550 and 1700. Rather than being discouraged by the various bans on playing passed by parliament during the interregnum,[10] publishers seemingly saw an opportunity to satisfy the appetite for plays, unquestionably whetted by the closed theaters, by increasing their availability in print. Richard Brome remarked how the theaters' closing worked "*to th' Stationers gaines*," and he assumed it would continue "*till some After-age / Shall put down Printing, as this doth the Stage.*"[11]

Perhaps surprisingly, Shakespeare was not among the most popular of the published dramatists in this period. As the theaters were closed, new plays contributed little to the publishers' offerings of printed drama, but, even among the Tudor and Stuart playwrights whose plays were newly printed, Shakespeare figures relatively inconsequentially. Only three editions of his plays were published during the interregnum – *Merchant of Venice* (1652), *King Lear* (1655), and *Othello* (1655). What must be granted is that Shakespeare's popularity had waned; other playwrights, most obviously, Beaumont and Fletcher (who had succeeded Shakespeare as the chief dramatists for the King's men) dominated the bookstalls.[12] A large folio collection of thirty-four of their plays, limited to those not otherwise in print, was published in 1647; and seventeen quartos of other plays by them were published between 1640 and 1660.

In 1652, Peter Heylyn, in an account of the state of English letters, judged Beaumont and Fletcher as "not inferiour unto *Terence* and *Plautus*" and considered his "friend Ben. Iohnson" as the "equall to any of the antients for the exactness of his pen";[13] but Shakespeare received no mention at all. The Rev. John Ward, vicar at Holy Trinity in Stratford, was quick to defend the honor of his fellow townsman, wondering whether Heylyn did "well in Reckoning up ye the Dramatick poets . . . To omit Shakespear,"[14] but the omission was not uncharacteristic of the age. In spite of being orthographically updated by the second folio, Shakespeare seemed to many distant and old-fashioned. The same year as Heylyn's slight, three publishers appended a note to an edition of Fletcher's *The Wild-Goose Chase*, offering, if there was sufficient public demand, "to bring Ben Johnson's two volumes into one, and publish them in this form; and also to reprint old Shakespear."[15] In the event it would wait another eleven years for sufficient interest to justify a new edition of "old Shakespear," but the adjective is telling, and like the limited seventeenth-century publication history that reflects it, gives the lie to Jonson's oft-quoted claim that Shakespeare was "not of an age but for all time."

At least in the second half of the seventeenth century, Shakespeare was clearly something less than the transcendent artist that later ages have loved not much, if at all, this side idolatry. Though highly praised, he is indeed "old Shakespear," a time-bound literary figure, very much of his age. New editions of the folio were eventually issued in 1663 and 1685, testifying to the continued existence of an interest in Shakespeare's works, but Shakespeare, however much admired, increasingly seemed dated. The new editions continued the project of modernizing spelling and grammar, making Shakespeare at least look contemporary on the page, but the plays were valued most often as the progenitors of the literary culture rather than as its finest exemplars. James Drake, defending Shakespeare and the stage against Jeremy Collier's charge of their immorality, calls Shakespeare "the *Proto-Dramatist* of *England*," though finding that he "fell short of the Art of *Jonson* and the Conversation of *Beaumont* and *Fletcher*."[16]

On the stage, the widening gap between Shakespeare's art and contemporary taste was unmistakable. There Shakespeare was not merely modernized, as he was on the printed page, but aggressively modified to satisfy the expectations of the fashionable audiences that filled the theaters, newly opened in the summer of 1660 after the eighteen-year official hiatus; and it is the most radical of the alterations that have, at least, retrospectively come to represent Restoration England's relation to Shakespeare.[17]

Changeable scenery and mechanical devices, *entr'acte* musical entertainment, and plots and idiom that were regularized and refined tamed Shakespeare's wild fancy to the service of a new sensibility. Characters were polarized, motivations untangled, morality clarified, song and spectacle amplified, and Shakespeare's language simplified and sophisticated. If Shakespeare was part of that giant race before the flood, he was no less an anachronism for his massive presence. What John Evelyn said of *Hamlet* in 1661 might have been said of any of Shakespeare's originals – "the old playe began to disgust this refined age"[18] – and the theater community worked hard to produce a Shakespeare that the "refined age" might more readily accept and admire.

We are all familiar with the process. Shakespeare's excellence is repeatedly gestured at but finally subordinated to different standards of taste. Dryden, for example, can assert that "Shakespear's pow'r is sacred as a King's" but also complain that Shakespeare's "whole stile is so pester'd with Figurative expressions, that it is as affected as it is obscure" and feel perfectly free, as in his *Troilus and Cressida*, to rewrite the play nominally to highlight "the admirable Genius of the Author." To that stated end, Dryden admits that he "new model'd the Plot," "threw out many unnecessary characters" and "improv'd" others whose lineaments had been promisingly begun; "with no small trouble" reordered the scenes so "that there is a coherence of 'em with one another"; and refined Shakespeare's language, drawing "his English nearer to our times."[19] The few plays that did survive largely unadapted – *Hamlet, 1 Henry IV, Julius Caesar, Othello, Henry VIII* – still unmistakably became Restoration drama on the stage. They were performed heavily cut (the originals "too long to be conveniently Acted," as the explanatory note to the 1676 edition of *Hamlet* says), with music and scenic effects added, and always with Shakespeare's language (as our editors might say) silently modernized.

Even as the new editions of the folio were issued in 1663 and 1685, Shakespeare was thriving in the theater, but only by having his texts reshaped according to aesthetic standards largely irrelevant and inhospitable to the originals. The alterations were made with no commitment to the intentions of Shakespeare's originals and with little, if any, embarrassment about their violation. Like Dryden, Nahum Tate, for example, happily admits to his "Newmodelling" of *King Lear*, which allows Cordelia to marry Edgar, and Lear to survive and look forward to being "Cheer'd with relation of the prosperous reign / Of this celestial pair" (5.6.151–2). The rending logic of Shakespeare's play is abandoned in Tate's comforting alteration, and perhaps the happy ending is as much topically, as aesthetically, motivated.[20] If the play is indeed a dramatic version of Tory providentialism, a compositorial error provides a breath-taking example of the play's political unconscious: Edgar's grief at seeing "the poor old King bareheaded / And drenched in this foul storm" (3.3.39–40) appears in all five of the early quartos of the play as a lament for the "poor old King *be*headed" (sig. E3ᵛ; Fig. 18). But happy endings need not necessarily point at the monarchy's restoration; even *Romeo and Juliet* was given a happy ending, "preserving Romeo and Juliet alive," and "Playd Alternatively, Tragical one Day, and Tragicomical another," as John Downes recalls.[21]

Tate admits to being "Rackt with no small Fears for so bold a Change" to Shakespeare's *Lear*, but he was relieved when he "found it well receiv'd by my Audience" (*History of King Lear*, sig. [A3ʳ]); and, as is well known, Tate's version continued to be "well receiv'd" for 150 years following its introduction. "In the present case," as Dr. Johnson said, "the public has decided," though Steevens rushed to correct his elder collaborator: "Dr. Johnson should rather have said that the managers of the theatres-royal have decided, and the public has been obliged to acquiesce in their decision."[22] But whoever was ultimately responsible, Shakespeare survived on the Restoration stage, but primarily in versions, as George Colman proudly stated in 1768, that had "been refined from the dross that hindered them."[23]

Later generations would be less happy with these refinements. "Those who believe in the high and serious calling of literary criticism will be disappointed," laments Brian Vickers, "that so many intelligent men and women who cared about Shakespeare and the drama failed to stop the 'new-modeling' of his plays."[24] Indeed, "Tatification" became a term of contempt in the mid-nineteenth

30   KING LEAR.

ſharp Haw-thorn blows the cold Wind —— Mum, Go to thy
Bed and warm Thee. —— ha! what do I ſee? by all my Griefs
the poor old King beheaded,   [*Aſide.*
And drencht in this ſow Storm, profeſſing *Syren,*
Are all your Proteſtations come to this?

   Lear. Tell me, Fellow, diſt thou give all to thy Daughters?

   Edg. Who gives any thing to poor *Tom ,* whom the foul
Fiend has led through Fire and through Flame, through Buſhes
and Boggs, that has laid Knives under his Pillow, and Halters
in his Pue, that has made him proud of Heart to ride on a Bay-
trotting Horſe over four inch'd Bridges, to courſe his own Sha-
dow for a Traytor. —bleſs thy five Wits, *Tom*'s a cold [*Shivers.*]
bleſs thee from Whirlwinds, Star-blaſting and Taking: do poor
Tom ſome Charity, whom the foul Fiend vexes—— Sa, ſa, there
I could have him now, and there, and there agen.

   Lear. Have his Daughters brought him to this paſs?
Cou'dſt thou ſave Nothing? didſt thou give 'em All?

   Kent. He has no Daughters, Sir.

   Lear. Death, Traytor, nothing cou'd have ſubdu'd Nature
To ſuch a Lowneſs but his unkind Daughters.

   Edg. Pillicock ſat upon Pillicock Hill; Hallo, hallo, hallo.

   Lear. Is it the faſhion that diſcarded Fathers
Should have ſuch little Mercy on their Fleſh?
Iudicious puniſhment, 'twas this Fleſh begot
Thoſe Pelican Daughters.

   Edg. Take heed of the ſow Fiend, obey thy Parents, keep
thy Word juſtly, Swear not, commit not with Man's ſworn
Spouſe, ſet not thy ſweet Heart on proud Array: *Tom*'s a Cold.

   Lear. What haſt thou been?

   Edg. A Serving-man proud of Heart, that curl'd my Hair,
us'd Perfume and Waſhes, that ſerv'd the Luſt of my Miſtreſſes
Heart, and did the Act of Darkneſs with her. Swore as many
Oaths as I ſpoke Words, and broke 'em all in the ſweet Face of
Heaven: Let not the Paint, nor the Patch, nor the ruſhing of
Silks betray thy poor Heart to Woman, keep thy Foot out of
Brothels, thy Hand out of Plackets, thy Pen from Creditors
Books, and defie the foul Fiend —— ſtill through the Haw-
thorn blows the cold Wind —— Seſs, Suum, Mun, Nonny,
                                                      Dolphin

18. Nahum Tate, *King Lear* (1681), sig. E3^v

century as Shakespeare's original texts began to return to the stage. The word was H. N. Hudson's dismissive coinage; and Hudson rose to rhetorical heights to register his dismay with the almost inescapable adaptations, referring to Tate's *Lear* as "this shameless, this execrable piece of dementation," and then, Lear-like, passionately calling down curses upon the impious practitioners: "Withered be the hand, palzied be the arm, that ever dares touch one of Shakespeare's plays."[25]

But "Shakespeare's plays" did not haughtily declare *noli me tangere*. Shakespeare survived precisely by being accessible and pliant in the hands of his lovers. The plays were decidedly aging beauties, and remained objects of desire only when dressed in youthful costume. Hudson's outrage presumes that Shakespeare's texts remain unwithered by age and unstaled by custom; and, if later ages have indeed often held it so, in the century and a half following the restoration of the monarchy they seemed more than a bit shopworn and unquestionably in need of a make-over. No discourtesy was intended. Indeed there is some evidence that adaptation was a badge of honor: in 1711 the edition of the *Works* of Beaumont and Fletcher insists that "three such extraordinary Writers as Mr. *Waller*, the Duke of *Buckingham*, and *John*, late Earl of *Rochester*, selecting each of them one of their Plays to alter for the Stage, adds not a little to their Reputation."[26] Shakespeare's texts were plays to be performed and had always yielded to the exigencies of theatrical necessity. The adaptations were serious and respectful efforts to make the excellence of the old plays visible to the new age. Dryden even found classical precedent for altering Shakespeare in the practice in Sophoclean Athens to give "an equal reward" to those able effectively to modernize Aeschylus for the stage and to those "whose productions were wholly new, and of their own."[27]

Considered as theatrical scripts, Shakespeare's texts received the precise treatment they requested. They were modified – as indeed they always had been – to play successfully on the stages of the time. Shakespeare's oft-remarked genius did not inhibit the impulse to adaptation; rather, in effect, it demanded the effort to make the plays acceptable to the new audiences that assembled in the theaters. "What are the lays of artful Addison, / Coldly correct, to Shakespeare's warblings wild," demanded Joseph Warton in 1700 in a familiar conceit,[28] but the very term of praise justified the cavalier treatment in the theater: Shakespeare's "warblings wild" needed to be tamed before they could be fully admired by the polite audiences of the day. The original texts, however valuable, were inevitably flawed, since they were written at a time when, as was often claimed, the "Public Taste was in its Infancy."[29]

Nonetheless, it is worth recalling, amidst the almost reflexive condescension that marks responses to Restoration Shakespeare, that Shakespeare seems to have returned to the stage, not in the sophisticated adaptations in which the plays would usually be seen for the next 150 years, but in much the same form as they had left it in 1642. The first play of Shakespeare apparently lawfully performed after the official cessation of playing, a production of *Pericles* at the Cockpit by a company of players under the management of John Rhodes (formerly the wardrobe keeper at the Blackfriars Theatre, as John Downes records[30]), was unlikely to have differed much from the last recorded pre-war production of the play at the Globe in June 1631, though the mouldy tale of Pericles' restoration to power and happiness would have had new relevance in the political environment of the summer of 1660.

Almost immediately, of course, the new aesthetic standards and theatrical conventions of Restoration England did quickly come to reshape Shakespeare's plays, but these were applied as much out of necessity as out of artistic conviction. In December 1660, William Davenant appealed to the Lord Chamberlain for the right to perform twenty-one plays, including nine by Shakespeare; but rather than merely seeking permission for an expanded repertory for his company, Davenant promised an aesthetic reformation: "a proposition of reformeinge some of the most ancient Playes that were playd at Blackfriers and of makeinge them, fitt," as the Lord Chamberlain reported and cited as the basis of his allowance.[31]

Davenant's proposition, however, was motivated more by theatrical desperation than by aesthetic confidence. The crown's limit of two patent theaters presumably should have allowed the two acting companies large enough repertories to play successfully, but with few new plays ready following the long official closure of the theaters and almost all of the most popular plays of the previous age

belonging to Thomas Killigrew's King's company, which was recognized as the heir of the pre-war King's men, Davenant's
company had little with which to appeal to the audiences that
eagerly awaited the reopened theaters. Indeed Davenant's Duke's
men seem to have had exclusive rights to only two plays: *The
Changeling* and *The Bondman*.[32] Davenant's promise to reform and
make fit the drama seems less a function of some revolutionary aesthetic commitment than of a fundamental pragmatic consideration. Only with such a promise would Davenant's company gain
access to the repertory they needed to survive. The adaptations,
which many in subsequent ages have derided, were, in effect,
required of Davenant by law.

Theatrical necessity, then, drove Davenant to attempt his
reforms, though their particular character was perhaps inevitable
for the author of the operatic *Siege of Rhodes*. With the success they
achieved on stage, Davenant initiated the long divorce of
Shakespeare's plays from the aesthetic logic that had determined
their writing. Ironically, Davenant was regularly claimed as a direct
link to the Shakespearean original – as in John Downes's account
of Betterton, who was "Instructed in [the role of Henry VIII] by
Sir *William*, who had it from Old Mr. *Lowen*, that had his instructions from Mr. *Shakespear* himself";[33] or, even more radically, in the
widely circulated tale that Davenant was actually "the natural son
of Shakespeare," in the words of an eighteenth-century Drury
Lane prompter.[34]

But whether or not Davenant was the illegitimate offspring of
Shakespeare's loins, he was no respectful child of Shakespeare's
theatrical imagination. Obviously he felt no obligation either to
Shakespeare's staging practices or to the structure or even the language of Shakespeare's texts. Davenant turned Shakespeare into a
contemporary playwright, at once modern and highbrow, fit for
the theatrical environment in which he was now performed.
Arguably it was this transformation that was responsible for
Shakespeare's survival in the repertory. "Old Shakespear" was
made new, and in his contemporary dress he filled the theaters.
Davenant's adaptations gave rise to more than fifty others in the
next hundred years. Only slowly did the fashion wane. But even if
few new adaptations were written after the 1780s, the old ones still

stubbornly remained in the repertory, keeping Shakespeare's own texts off the stage for a remarkable length of time: as Jean Marsden reminds us, "Tate's *Lear* appeared until 1836, Garrick's *Catherine and Petruchio* until 1887, and elements of his *Romeo and Juliet* until 1884."[35]

It was not, however, only the theater professionals who appropriated Shakespeare for an alien aesthetic, as they sought to keep him "fresh and fair" (*Troilus and Cressida*, 4.5.1). Even Lewis Theobald was willing to alter Shakespeare for the stage, on exactly the same principles on which his predecessors in adaptation had operated. "The many scatter'd Beauties," which he had "long admir'd" in *Richard II*, "induc'd [him] to think they would have stronger Charms if they were interwoven in a regular fable . . . maintaining the *Unity* of *Action* and supporting the *Dignity* of the *Characters*."[36] The prologue spoken in the theater announces that "Immortal *Shakespear* on this tale began, / And wrote it in a rude, Historick plan, / On this rich fund our Author builds his Play / Keeps all his Gold, and throws his Dross away" (sig. Bb3ʳ). The ambiguous pronouns register the complexities of textual authority: "his Gold" and "his Dross" are of course Shakespeare's, but "his play" is presumably Theobald's; he is "our author" who has chosen what to keep and what to discard in regularizing the play to fit the desired neo-classic norms.

What is most remarkable about this alteration, which is in most respects identical in style and motive to other Restoration and eighteenth-century adaptations, is that it is Theobald's. If anyone might be expected to respect Shakespeare's text it should be the man most publicly identified with the editorial effort to establish what Shakespeare had written. His exultant critique of Pope's edition in *Shakespeare Restored* (provoking Pope's contemptuous portrait of "piddling Tibbalds" in *The Dunciad*) announced his commitment to "restore, to the best of my Power, the Poet's true text."[37] But despite what he calls his "Veneration, almost rising to Idolatry, for the Writings" of Shakespeare (p. iii), his *Richard II* (admittedly performed some seven years before the publication of *Shakespeare Restored*) manages to retain only about one quarter of Shakespeare's text, and reassign some of that. "You have many happy years to come," Bolingbroke offers as consolation to the heartsick York, who has just learned of his son's death; "But not a Moment, King, that Thou canst give" (p. 48), York bitterly replies in the transposition (and slight rewriting) of Shakespeare's dialogue between Richard and Gaunt at 1.3.225–6. And Gaunt's great set piece on "this England" is shortened and transferred to Aumerle at the end of Theobald's play, as York's son is taken to his execution for his loyalty to Richard – and tellingly includes as an index of the play's own political moment the unshakespearean epithet "This Land of Liberty" (p. 54).[38]

Theobald's play is, however, as much about love as about politics. His Richard is more like Shakespeare's Antony than Shakespeare's Angevin King, quick to renounce the claims of political responsibility for those of the heart. At the end of act one, the evidence of Queen Isabella's devoted love leads him to abandon his commitment to the "ostentation of despised Empire" (p. 11). "Crowns shall no more from Love my Thought's divide," announces Richard, leaving the political world to the ambitious Bolingbroke and taking solace in the "partnership of lasting Sorrow" his Queen offers him (p. 27). Richard is fatally stabbed as he and his Queen are parted – "They shall not force thee from me" – and he dies with Isabella's name upon his lips (pp. 58–9). In performance, Isabella, played by Mrs. Bullock, spoke an epilogue, protesting that she was sent off to France having been allowed no adequate expression of her grief: "He should have made me like lamenting Dido," she complains, and she directly addresses the women in the audience, offering her enduring love for Richard to motivate the *plaudite*:

> Dear ladies, do not make the case your own:
> What e'er by Tragick scenes the Bard intends,
> I'll Swear, that he and I will ne'er be Friends,
> Till he can place me by his Magick Pen
> In *Statu quo*, and marry me again.
> But, for my sake, not that the Bard may thrive,
> Give your Leave, that *Richard* may revive.

(sig. Bb4ʳ)

Whatever can be said about Theobald's *Richard II*, it is unquestionably an Augustan play in style, form, and motive. The "innovations upon History and Shakespear" (sig. Aa1ʳ), which Theobald proudly acknowledges, purposefully shape the plot to create something far from the design of Shakespeare's history. The monarchical politics of Shakespeare's play survive, if at all, in residual registers of the trauma of Charles I's execution, as in the play's final couplet: "Tho Vengeance may a while withhold her Hand, / A King's Blood, unattone'd, must curse the Land" (p. 60). But the center of Theobald's play is in the non-Shakespearean intensities of the love plots, in Isabella's commitment to Richard and in Lady Percy's love for Aumerle. *Richard II* is revised for the tastes and interests of polite Augustan society and rewritten to exploit contemporary stagecraft, not least the talented actresses available to play the female roles.

But the specifics of Theobald's rather conventional adaptation are, at least for us, finally less important than that it exists at all. It must seem odd that the contemporary most committed to – and arguably most capable of – recovering Shakespeare's original text from the imperfections of the printed editions should so thoroughly alter one of Shakespeare's plays to satisfy the theater audiences of his own time. But in the single figure of Lewis Theobald can be seen the era's schizophrenic relation to Shakespeare – always admiring, but, in one mode, presumptuously altering his plays for success on the stage, while, in another, determinedly seeking the authentic text in the succession of scholarly editions that followed Rowe's. The title page of Theobald's alteration (Fig. 19) – if that is what it is[39] – of *Double Falsehood* economically makes the point, almost oxymoronically identifying it as "Written Originally by W. SHAKESPEARE; And now Revis'd and Adapted to the Stage By Mr. Theobald, the Author of *Shakespeare Restor'd*." Unsurprisingly, Theobald names himself on the title page as the adapter of the putatively Shakespearean play, but he contravenes that role by identifying himself as the author of a book that is committed, as he says, to "retrieving as far as possible, the *original Purity* of [Shakespeare's] *Text*" (*Shakespeare Restored*, sig. B1ʳ).

Theobald obviously felt no tension between the two roles, as reviser of Shakespeare and as his restorer, his amphibian contentment manifest not only on the title page of *Double Falsehood* but also in the very dedication of *Shakespeare Restored* to John Rich, not a fellow editor or a patron committed to their project, but the

Double Falſhood;

OR,

The DISTREST LOVERS.

A

P L A Y,

As it is Acted at the

THEATRE-ROYAL

IN

D R U R Y-L A N E.

Written Originally by *W. SHAKESPEARE*;
And now Reviſed and Adapted to the Stage
By Mr. THEOBALD, the Author of *Shakeſpeare Reſtor'd.*

*———— Quod optanti Divûm promittere nemo
Auderet, volvenda Dies, en! attulit ultrò.*   Virg.

The SECOND EDITION.

L O N D O N:

Printed by J. WATTS, at the Printing-Office in
Wild-Court near *Lincolns-Inn Fields.*

M DCC XXVIII.

19. Lewis Theobald, *Double Falsehood* (1728), title page

manager at Lincoln's Inn and the inventor of the popular panto-mimes. Theobald playfully calls him "a Sinner against Shakespeare" (sig. A3^r) for the careless treatment Shakespeare received in his theater, but agrees to forgive his friend's theatrical transgressions. "The Taste of the Publick demands it of you," Theobald concedes, and he looks to a time when "their palates alter" (sig. A3^r) and Shakespeare can be restored to the stage as well as to the printed page. But it would be another century before the adaptations would disappear from the theater. Through the 1720s, Shakespeare continued to be adapted – Aaron Hill's *Henry V*, Ambrose Phillips's *2 Henry VI*, Dennis's *Coriolanus*, Cibber's (prob-ably unplayed) *King John* – and many of the earlier altered versions were still successfully being played. Shakespeare kept his hold on the playhouse primarily in altered forms, at the same time that his original texts were being aggressively pursued in the study. On stage, Shakespeare's words were free to be rearranged, refined and revised, all in the service of keeping them current; on the page, in a different spirit of adulation, they were to be restored to their authentic form.

Clearly this would not be the last time that theatrical practice and scholarly activity would be at odds, though arguably the diver-gence would never be more extreme. Shakespeare on stage assumed ever stranger shapes, not only in the modifications of the text but in the totality of the theatrical event in which it was embedded. For example, a production of *Macbeth* on 5 May 1726 at Drury Lane advertised the play as "Written by Shakespear" but is in fact (as usual) the Davenant version "with all Songs, Dances, and other Decorations proper to the Play," which apparently included a muzette, a children's wooden shoe dance, a pantomime enacted in whiteface, and a full Corelli concerto played after the second act.[40] Shakespeare is not merely adapted on stage but diluted in such evening's entertainment, though his name increas-ingly comes to legitimize the dilutions.[41]

But it was not the depredations that Shakespeare endured on the stage that provoked the eighteenth-century editors working to recover and restore Shakespeare's original texts. Plays, it was assumed, *would* be adapted for the theater. The successive editions of Shakespeare's *Works* (and the title of these multi-volume editions is not insignificant, speaking the literary assumptions of the editorial work[42]) sought not to rescue him from the appropriations of the theater but, in Rowe's words, "to redeem him from the Injuries of former Impressions" (sig. A2^r). The Shakespeare that the editors served was explicitly an author not a playwright, and his plays, for their purposes, were, therefore, not scripts to be performed (and thus inevitably to be modified) but plays to be read (and thus demanding a correct and stable text). For them the task was to establish a text as close as possible to what Shakespeare himself had put on paper, recovering it from the imperfect record of the surviving printed editions.

There were, of course, published editions that did attempt to register and exploit the plays' theatrical existence. Individually printed plays were offered for sale with the phrase, "now published as it is performed at the Theatres Royal" authorizing the text for readers, just as the phrase, "as it was publicly acted," had graced title pages of printed plays in the late sixteenth century. In 1773 (not insignificantly as discussions in the House of Lords about the meaning of the 1709 copyright act were nearing a conclusion[43]), a collection of such editions was published in nine duodecimo volumes by John Bell, claiming that the printed texts reflected the plays "as they are now performed in the Theatres Royal in London; Regulated from the Prompt Books of each House By Permission." Clearly there was a market for such texts, though even contemporaries recognized their limitations. J. P. Genest, in 1832, commented that Bell's collection was widely "censured as the worst edition of Shakespeare ever published; which *strictly* speaking is true, as it presents the play in a mutilated state."[44] The "mutilations" no doubt record some aspect of contemporary theatrical practice (and were, and remain, of interest precisely for that reason), but their close connection to the theater is precisely what determined their irrelevance to the age's sustained editorial project of establishing Shakespeare's genuine text.[45]

If Shakespeare was a contemporary on stage, subject to the dramatic standards of the age and the inevitable contingent demands of performance, on the page he "stands, or at least ought to stand," as Theobald argues, "in the nature of a classic Writer" (*Shakespeare Restored*, p. v), worthy of having the corruptions worked by theatrical necessity, printing practice, and time recognized and repaired. The plays, rescued from their Restoration appropriations, increasingly became a kind of secular scripture – not, of course, the divine Word but the words of the "divine *Shakespeare*," as Dryden seems to be the first to call him.[46] Once praised as "sweet," "mellifluous," or "ingenious" (even "copious," as the bookman Francis Kirkman understandably said, listing forty-eight plays "by" Shakespeare in his 1671 catalogue), Shakespeare becomes "immortal" and "Godlike," himself a "kind of established religion," as Arthur Murphy said in 1753, his works "a lay bible."[47]

Even before Shakespeare's full cultural theogony in the 1750s, the language of religious engagement had already begun to surround the texts of the plays, and, as Marcus Walsh and Simon Jarvis have convincingly shown, knowledge of debates in biblical criticism affected the approach to Shakespeare's text.[48] Pope spoke of his own "religious Abhorrence of Innovation" in justifying his reluctance to emend the deficiencies of the plays he came to edit, while Theobald similarly claimed that he "religiously adher'd" to the "genuine Text" of the plays.[49] Nonetheless, Theobald denied that "we ought to be as cautious of altering *their* Text, as we would That of the *sacred Writings*," but almost immediately blurred the distinction he proposed: the Bible itself has "admitted of some Thousands of various Readings," continues Theobald, "and would have a great many more, had not Dr. *BENTLEY* some particular Reasons for not prosecuting his Undertaking upon the New Testament, as he propos'd" (*Shakespeare Restored*, p. iv), recognizing the applicability of the example to his own project. Even the holy word of God was in need of editorial attention, and the editors of Shakespeare's plays increasingly accepted as an article of faith, one might say, that if the biblical word might be restored by the application of systematic techniques of textual criticism so might the text that Mary Cowden Clarke would in 1829 call "the bible of the intellectual world."[50]

Michael Dobson, among others, has brilliantly explored this process of Shakespeare's cultural elevation.[51] Unlike Dobson, however, I am interested here less in the ideological motives of bardolatry than in its textual effects. As old Shakespeare is slowly converted into our Shakespeare, everybody's Shakespeare, the desire to recover the lost perfection of his text becomes ever more intense. The eighteenth-century editors, each in turn, enacted what Theobald would call their "Hopes of restoring to the Publick their greatest Poet in his Original Purity" (*Works*, 1733, vol. 1, p. xxxix), yet from the very beginning the difficulty of fully realizing those hopes was recognized. Shakespeare did become a book to be read and valued. "The Author is grown so universal a Book, that there are very few Studies or Collections of Books, tho' small, amongst which it does not hold a place" (*Shakespeare Restored*, pp. v-vi), as Theobald says, apparently coining the now familiar metonym, though it is implicit in Heminge and Condell's instruction in the 1623 Shakespeare folio to "Reade *him*, therefore; and againe, and againe" (sig. A3^r, emphasis mine). But it was immediately apparent that "Shakespeare" was a book whose text could not be definitively established.

Nicholas Rowe's edition of 1709, the first of the eighteenth-century editions, was published with some fanfare by Jacob Tonson. *The London Gazette* advertised it as "a very neat and correct edition of Mr. William Shakespeare's work in six volumes in octavo, adorned with cuts."[52] "Neat" it was, its octavo volumes certainly easier to handle than the large fourth folio that it replaced, but the limits of its correctness were obvious even to its editor. "I must not pretend to have restor'd this Work to the Exactness of the Author's Original Manuscripts," writes Rowe: "Those are lost, or, at least are gone beyond any Inquiry I could make; so that there was nothing left, but to compare the several Editions, and give the true Reading as well I could from thence."[53] Rowe, in fact, compared somewhat fewer of the "several Editions" than he claimed, basing his own edition (for which he was paid £36 10s) almost entirely on the fourth folio, the rights to which Tonson had purchased from Henry Henningman,[54] and collating only a few late seventeenth-century quartos (recovering and restoring, for example, the prologue to *Romeo and Juliet*). But the very fact that Rowe at least understood that Shakespeare's intentions could only be partially recovered from the surviving print record, combined with his stated, if unfulfilled, commitment to compare early editions rather than merely assuming the authority of the folio he worked from, established the basic conditions for editing Shakespeare that still pertain.[55]

In 1721, seven years after the publication of the second edition of Rowe's work, *Mist's Journal* announced that "the celebrated Mr. Pope is preparing a correct edition of Shakespeare's works; that of the late Mr. Rowe being very faulty."[56] In his effort to remedy the limitations of Rowe's text, Pope examined many more of the early textual witnesses than the few late quartos that Rowe had consulted. In October 1721, Pope and Tonson advertised for "old Editions of single Plays,"[57] and Pope eventually saw early quartos of eighteen of the nineteen plays for which a pre-folio printing exists (all except *Much Ado*), twenty-nine in all, though only six were first editions. Pope examined these carefully, convening, as he told his publisher, "Parties of my acquaintance ev'ry night, to collate the several Editions of Shakespear's single Plays."[58] Even as his edition reached completion, he continued to seek more early printings of the plays, although the terms of the appeal itself revealed the limited state of bibliographic knowledge. In May 1722, advertisements were placed: "The new edition of Shakespeare being now in the press; this is to give notice that if any person has editions of *The Tempest, Macbeth, Julius Caesar, Timon of Athens, King John,* and *Henry the Eighth* printed before 1620 and will communicate the same to J. Tonson in the Strand, he shall receive satisfaction required."[59]

Nothing could have come of that solicitation – all the sought-after plays, of course, having been printed for the first time only in the 1623 folio – but it reveals the genuine desire to fill in the gaps of the early history of Shakespeare in print. "It is impossible to repair the Injuries already done Him," Pope writes, "too much time has elaps'd and the materials are too few," but Pope strove to thicken the bibliographic record, aware that it offers "the only materials left to repair the deficiencies or restore the corrupted sense of the Author" (*Works*, 1725, vol. 1, pp. xxii–xxiii).

Pope did not, of course, achieve a "correct" edition of Shakespeare's works, any more than did Rowe. Pope conceived of his editorial task more as mediation than remediation: Shakespeare was made fit for Augustan readers. Unsurprisingly, the edition, published in 1725, is now best remembered for its conspicuous impositions of contemporary taste upon Shakespeare's text: in the regularizing of the verse, in distinguishing "the most shining passages" by marking them with commas in the margins, and, most notoriously, in identifying "suspected passages, which are excessively bad," and which are, therefore, "degraded to the bottom of the page" (*Works*, 1725, vol. 1, pp. xxii–xxiii). Some 1,500 lines are thus degraded.

But although Pope's relatively extensive knowledge of the early printings, then, seemingly served more to authorize his omissions than to restore Shakespeare's text (Johnson said of Pope that "he rejected whatever he disliked and thought more of amputation than of cure"[60]), it is arguably Pope's aggressive pursuit of the early print history – and his appreciation of "the drudgery of comparing impressions" – for which his editorial work should be remembered.[61] His use of this material was no doubt unsystematic and willful, at best serving as a repository of attractive readings without any clear conception of how the usually derivative relation of the various editions would affect the authority of the later texts; but his recognition and articulation of its crucial importance, evidenced not least by his inclusion of "a Catalogue of those first [*sic*] Editions by which the greater part of the various readings and of the corrected passages are authorised" (*Works*, 1725, vol. 1, p. xxii), mark the beginnings of a historically based editorial practice, as they also mark the beginning of an editorial tradition largely hostile to the theater, assuming its task to be as much the rescue of Shakespeare's texts from their vitiation by "the ignorance of the Players, both as his actors, and his editors" as from "the many blunders and illiteracies of the first Publishers of his works" (*Works*, 1725, vol. 1, p. xiv).

If Pope did recognize the value of the early editions, he was far better at collecting than collating them, and it would wait for Theobald in fact to set editing upon a truly historical footing.[62] Theobald was the Tonson firm's next chosen editor (receiving over £600 for his effort, plus 400 copies on Genoa paper and another 100 on Royal, the looming expiration of Tonson's Shakespeare copyright no doubt driving up Theobald's price[63]), and like his predecessors he prepared his edition from the latest Tonson-owned offering. His edition, published first in 1733, was prepared from Pope's second edition of 1728, though he correctly included Pope's editions, along with Rowe's, among the "Editions of no authority" in his table of editions collated.[64] This seeming contradiction has often been used to prove a fundamental muddle-headedness in his approach, but in fact, Theobald's decision to edit from Pope's text was, like Rowe's to work from the fourth folio, and Pope from Rowe's, a function both of convenience and copyright. It was, of course, an edition easily at hand, but more importantly the Tonson family used its publication of the successive editions, each based upon its predecessor, to assert its continued copyright of the text itself.[65]

Presumably, then, Theobald had little choice in the matter of where he started, but he understood the necessity of returning to the earliest texts to establish the true readings. Johnson takes him to task for considering the second folio equally with the first as an edition of "high" authority in this effort and for considering the third even as an edition of "middle authority," since, as Johnson says, only the first is consequential, "the rest only deviat[ing] from it by the printers' negligence."[66] Theobald, however, had already grasped this fundamental point, affirming as a basic principle, that "the more the Editions of any Book multiply, the more the Errors multiply too, and propagate out of their own Species" (*Shakespeare Restored*, pp. ii–iii). When he turned to later, derivative editions, it was not in some naive belief that they were of equal authority with the first, but, rather, in the plausible conviction that they were closer to the linguistic environment of the original than he was, and so their efforts to make sense of an obscure or deficient text had some greater likelihood of being correct than a modern editor's guesses or even the first printer's hurried composition. More than any previous editor, and more than most of his successors, Theobald understood how editions followed from one another, recognizing (if not always following) the implications of their development and often deterioration "thro' the whole Chain of Impressions" (*Works*, 1733, vol. 4, p. 413).

Conscientious, often to the point of pedantry, Theobald's usually careful, if not completely systematic, collation of early texts did allow him to develop both a theory of the plays' textual transmission and a methodology of textual correction, which, although admittedly deficient in some aspects, nonetheless often surprisingly anticipate what the new bibliography would make normative for the twentieth century. Theobald understood the imperfections of the existing copies and was willing to correct their deficiencies, emending "against all the Copies" if necessary, though he was committed "never to alter at all" where he was able to "explain a passage into sense."[67] Where emendation was necessary, it was to be based on a familiarity with the author's lexographic and literary habits, but knowledge also of what Greg would call "the concrete familiarities of the theatre, the scrivener's shop, and the printing house."[68]

Certainly more than any of his contemporaries, Theobald had made those familiarities his own. If he was, nonetheless, aware that "the want of *Originals* reduces us to the necessity of *guessing*, in order to amend" the text (*Shakespeare Restored*, p. 133), he was willing to "flatter" himself that his "Emendations are so far from being arbitrary and capricious, that They are establish'd with a very high Degree of moral Certainty" (*Works*, 1733, vol. 1, p. xlii). And if that willingness to flatter himself must be recognized as both over-confident and all too characteristic, Theobald must be given credit for freeing the project of editing Shakespeare from the capriciousness of literary taste.

Although the two editions of Theobald's Shakespeare (1733 and 1740, as well as a small run reprint of the 1733 edition published in Dublin in 1739) brought him little of the satisfaction he sought, his reputation almost permanently sullied by Pope's lampoon (and its later echoes by Warburton and Johnson) and the edition never providing enough of the money he hoped for, much of the editorial work he did has lasted and has increasingly found admirers. Henry Fielding was among those who immediately saw its value, and in a verse epistle he turned on Pope, extravagantly praising Theobald's achievement:

> His name with Shakespeare's shall to Ages Soar
> When thou shalt jingle in our Ears no more;
> Shakespeare by him restor'd again we see
> Recover'd of the Wounds he bore from thee.
> And sure brighter must his Merit shine
> Who gives us Sha[kes]peare's Works, than his who thine.[69]

If Fielding's enthusiastic judgment has been belied by literary history, still it is true, as Peter Alexander writes, that "there is no modern edition of Shakespeare that does not include many of the happy suggestions first proposed by Theobald."[70]

Subsequent editors would build on what Theobald had begun, but it is a mistake to see the editorial history as the record of a gradual but inevitable progress towards, in Margreta de Grazia's phrase for the object of editorial desire, "the authentic text, the text closest to what Shakespeare put on paper."[71] Hanmer, Warburton, Johnson, Capell, Steevens, Malone, Boswell, men more or less talented, knowledgeable, and industrious, each in turn did add to what was known about what Shakespeare had written and how his texts were transmitted. "Not one has left Shakespeare without improvement," generously concluded Johnson of his predecessors,[72] but the editions cannot be seen as steady steps towards the perfecting of Shakespeare's text.

This is not, however, to side with de Grazia in seeing editorial sophistication as an epistemological rupture (whether that rupture takes place with Malone, as de Grazia argues, or with Capell, or with Theobald, or with . . .), against the claims for the aggregated editorial accomplishment of the age. It is, instead, to see in that very aggregation the evidence of the resistant uncertainties of the text that it sought to resolve. Indeed the text, rather than appearing ever more uniform and firmly authorized, increasingly reveals itself as a shifting and sharply contested terrain. As the authentic Shakespeare was sought with ever greater confidence – Warburton, for example, claiming on the title page of his edition of 1747 (Fig. 20) that "The Genuine Text (collated with all the former Editions, and then corrected and emended) is here settled" – the succession of editions in fact declared the indeterminate nature of the project, the next edition required to address the failings of the last.

Even on the printed page the instability of Shakespeare's text declared itself. The virtually plain text of Rowe gave way to pages where the editorial involvement is increasingly visible and important (Figs. 21 and 22), culminating in the variorum editions of Johnson, Steevens, and Isaac Reed. The commentary and other apparatus sharing the page with Shakespeare's words made the uncertainties about Shakespeare's text unmistakable, and, worse, as Richard Porson said, threatened to make the text itself "only an

THE
WORKS
OF
SHAKESPEAR

IN EIGHT VOLUMES.

The Genuine Text (collated with all the former
Editions, and then corrected and emended)
is here fettled:

Being reftored from the *Blunders* of the firft Editors,
and the *Interpolations* of the two Laft:

WITH

A Comment and Notes, Critical and Explanatory.

By Mr. POPE *and Mr.* WARBURTON.

——Quorum omnium Interpretes, ut Grammatici, Poetarum
proximè ad eorum, quos interpretantur, divinationem vi-
dentur accedere.   *Cic. de Divin.*

Ἡ ΤΩΝ ΛΟΓΩΝ ΚΡΙΣΙΣ ΠΟΛΛΗΣ ΕΣΤΙ ΠΕΙΡΑΣ
ΤΕΛΕΥΤΑΙΟΝ ΕΠΙΓΕΝΝΗΜΑ.   *Long. de Sublim.*

LONDON:

Printed for *J.* and *P. Knapton, S. Birt, T. Longman* and
T. Shewell, H. Lintott, C. Hitch, J. Brindley, J. and *R. Ton-
fon* and *S. Draper, R. Wellington, E. New,* and *B. Dod.*

MDCCXLVII.

20. William Warburton (ed.) *The Works of Shakespear* (1747), title page

of King Henry IV. 1177

Bard. Yea, two and two, *Newgate* Fashion.

Hoft. My Lord, I pray you hear me.

P. Henry. What fay'ft thou, Miftrefs *Quickly*? How does thy Husband? I love him well, he is an honeft Man.

Hoft. Good, my Lord, hear me.

Fal. Prithee let her alone, and lift to me.

P. Henry. What fay'ft thou, *Jack*?

Fal. The other Night I fell afleep here behind the Arras, and had my Pocket pickt: This Houfe is turn'd Bawdy-houfe, they pick Pockets.

P. Henry. What didft thou lofe, *Jack*?

Fal. Wilt thou believe me, *Hal*? Three or four Bonds of forty Pound a piece, and a Seal-Ring of my Grandfather's.

P. Henry. A Trifle, fome eight-penny Matter.

Hoft. So I told him, my Lord; and I faid, I heard your Grace fay fo: And, my Lord, he fpeaks moft vilely of you, like a foul-mouth'd Man as he is, and faid he would cudgel you.

P. Henry. What, he did not?

Hoft. There's neither Faith, Truth, nor Woman-Hood in me elfe.

Fal. There's no more Faith in thee than in a ftew'd Prune; nor no more Truth in thee than in a drawn Fox; and for Woman-hood, Maid-Marian may be the Deputies Wife of the Ward to thee. Go you nothing, go.

Hoft. Say, what thing? What thing?

Fal. What thing? Why a thing to thank Heav'n on.

Hoft. I am nothing to thank Heav'n on, I would thou fhouldft know it: I am an honeft Man's Wife; and fetting thy Knighthood afide, thou art a Knave to call me fo.

Fal. Setting thy Womanhood afide, thou art a Beaft to fay otherwife.

Hoft. Say, what Beaft, thou Knave thou?

Fal. What Beaft? Why an Otter.

P. Henry. An Otter, Sir *John*, why an Otter?

Fal. Why? fhe's neither Fifh nor Flefh; a Man knows not where to have her.

Hoft. Thou art an unjuft Man in faying fo; thou, or any Man knows where to have me, thou Knave thou.

P. Henry.

21. *1 Henry IV*, in *The Works of Shakespeare*, ed. Nicholas Rowe (1709) vol. 3

362   FIRST PART OF

a drawn fox ;⁵ and for womanhood, maid Marian

two difhes of *ftewed prunes*, a bawd and a pander !" Again, in *Northward Hoe*, by Decker and Webfter, 1607, a bawd fays, " I will have but fix *ftewed prunes* in a difh, and fome of mother Wall's cakes ; for my beft cuftomers are tailors." Again, in *The Noble Stranger*, 1640 : " —— to be drunk with cream and *ftewed prunes* ! ——Pox on't, bawdy-houfe fare." Again, in Decker's *Seven deadly Sinnes of London*, 1606 ; " Nay, the fober Perpetuana-fuited Puritane, that dares not (fo much as by moone-light) come neare the fuburb fhadow of a houfe where they fet *ftewed prunes* before you, raps as boldly at the hatch, when he knows Candlelight is within, as if he were a new chofen conftable."

The paffages already quoted are fufficient to fhow that *a difh of ftewed prunes* was not only the ancient defignation of a brothel, but the conftant appendage to it.

From *A Treatife on the Lues Venerea*, written by W. Clowes, one of her majefty's furgeons, 1596, and other books of the fame kind, it appears that *prunes* were directed to be boiled in broth for thofe perfons already infected ; and that both *ftewed prunes* and roafted apples were commonly, though unfuccefsfully, taken by way of prevention. So much for the infidelity of *ftewed prunes*.
                                                STEEVENS.

Mr. Steevens has fo fully difcuffed the fubject of *ftewed prunes*, that one can add nothing but the *price*. In a piece called *Banks's Bay Horfe in a Trance*, 1595, we have " a ftock of wenches, fet up with their *ftewed prunes*, nine for a tefter."
                                                FARMER.

⁵ —— *a drawn fox* ;] A *drawn fox* may be a fox drawn over the ground, to exercife the hounds. So, in Beaumont and Fletcher's *Tamer Tamed* :
    " —— that *drawn fox* Morofo."

Mr. Heath obferves, that " a *fox drawn* over the ground to leave a fcent, and exercife the hounds, may be faid to have no truth in it, becaufe it deceives the hounds, who run with the fame eagernefs as if they were in purfuit of a real fox."

I am not, however, confident that this explanation is right. It was formerly fuppofed that a *fox*, when *drawn* out of his hole, had the fagacity to *counterfeit death*, that he might thereby obtain an opportunity to efcape. For this information I am indebted to Mr. Tollet, who quotes *Olaus Magnus*, Lib. XVIII. cap. xxxix : " Infuper finget fe mortuam," &c. This particular and many others relative to the fubtilty of the fox, have been tranflated by feveral ancient Englifh writers. STEEVENS.

KING HENRY IV.   363

may be the deputy's wife of the ward to thee.⁶ Go, you thing, go.

⁶ —— maid Marian *may be* &c.] *Maid Marian* is a man dreffed like a woman, who attends the dancers of the morris.
                                                JOHNSON.

In the ancient *Songs of Robin Hood* frequent mention is made of *maid Marian*, who appears to have been his concubine. I could quote many paffages in my old MS. to this purpofe, but fhall produce only one :
    " Good Robin Hood was living then,
    " Which now is quite forgot,
    " And fo was fayre *maid marian*," &c. PERCY.

It appears from the old play of *The Downfall of Robert Earl of Huntington*, 1601, that *maid Marian* was originally a name affumed by *Matilda* the daughter of *Robert Lord Fitzwater*, while *Robin Hood* remained in a ftate of outlawry :
    " Next 'tis agreed (if therto fhee agree)
    " That faire *Matilda* henceforth change her name ;
    " And while it is the chance of *Robin Hoode*
    " To live in Sherewodde a poor outlawes life,
    " She by *maide Marian's* name be only call'd.
    " *Mat.* I am contented ; reade on, little John :
    " Henceforth let me be nam'd *maide Marian*."

This lady was poifoned by King John at Dunmow Priory, after he had made feveral fruitlefs attempts on her chaftity. Drayton has written her legend.

Shakfpeare fpeaks of *maid Marian* in her degraded ftate, when fhe was reprefented by a ftrumpet or a clown.

See Figure 2, in the plate at the end of this play, with Mr. Tollet's obfervation on it. STEEVENS.

Maid Marian feems to have been the lady of a *Whitfun-ale*, or morris-dance. The Widow, in Sir W. D'Avenant's *Love and Honour*, (p. 247,) fays : " I have been *Miftrefs Marian* in a *Maurice* ere now." Morris is, indeed, there fpelt wrong ; the dance was not fo called from prince *Maurice*, but from the Spanifh *morifco*, a dancer of the *morris* or *moorifh* dance.
                                                HAWKINS.

There is an old piece entitled, *Old Meg of Herefordfhire for a Mayd-Marian, and Hereford Town for a Morris-dance ; or 12 Morris-dancers in Herefordfhire, of 1200 Years old.* Lond. 1609, quarto. It is dedicated to one Hall, a celebrated Tabourer in that country. T. WARTON.

---

22. "First Variorum," *Plays and Poems of William Shakespeare*, ed. (London, 1803), vol. 11, pp. 362–3

incidental object."[73] Though editors regularly insisted on the primacy of the plays over the notes, one reviewer observed that "a reader, at all inquisitive, can scarcely keep his eyes from them, and is frequently drawn into the whirlpool in spite of all his efforts."[74] An advertisement for the 1778 Johnson-Steevens edition visually makes the point with its three columns dominating the layout, each with seventeen names, printed in small capitals, of critics whose commentary is included (Fig. 23).

The scholarly project that had begun with the goal of establishing a "correct" text of Shakespeare's plays, which could be easily and confidently read in that knowledge, in fact produced a text in which arguments about its correctness were the very justification for its existence. If in the hands of the theater professionals Shakespeare's plays docilely yielded to the requirements of taste and fashion (even, it should be said, in Garrick's hands, who, while passionately declaring his commitments to the authentic text, in fact continued the theatrical traditions of textual alteration in the name of improvement[75]), in the hands of their editors, the plays grudgingly gave way before the academic disputes of the scholarly community. In spite of its obvious industry and intelligence, a century of critical attention had succeeded primarily in making the instabilities and imperfections of the text matters of common knowledge. Although some no doubt believed, as Ralph Griffiths claimed in 1773, that "the multiplicity of editions which his plays have undergone" testifies to "the high esteem in which the writings of Shakespeare are held," many more must have been persuaded, as Steevens himself realized, that "our author's text . . . on account of readings received and reprobated must remain in an unsettled state, and float in obedience to every gale of contradictory criticism."[76]

Perhaps it was this understanding that motivated an odd project of 1807. The firm of E. and J. Wright of St. Johns Square, London produced a reprint of the 1623 folio. Although unable accurately to duplicate the type fonts of the first edition, they carefully replicated the folio's design, layout, spelling, and foliation; and they printed the handsome facsimile on paper graced with a watermark of Shakespeare's name in block capitals. Learning of the project and recognizing its ambitions, Thomas Percy wrote Malone,

Lately Published,
In Ten Volumes, large Octavo,
(Price Three Pounds and Ten Shillings, bound)

THE
P L A Y S
OF
WILLIAM SHAKSPEARE,

With the CORRECTIONS and ILLUSTRATIONS of

ROWE,	FARMER,	TYRWHITT,
POPE,	PERCY,	MALONE,
THEOBALD,	TOLLET,	COLMAN,
HANMER,	HURD,	KENRICK,
WARBURTON,	HARDINGE,	REED,
UPTON,	HOLT,	FOLKES,
GREY,	GOLDSMITH,	LETHERLAND,
EDWARDS,	COLLINS,	BARRINGTON,
RODERICK,	BURROW,	JAMES,
THIRLBY,	SMITH,	RAWLINSON,
BISHOP,	CHAMIER,	BOWLE,
HEATH,	HAWKINS,	J. WARTON,
RIDLEY,	MUSGRAVE,	MURPHY,
SEYWARD,	LANGTON,	T. WARTON,
SYMPSON,	OLDYS,	WEST,
GRANGER,	GUTHRIE,	WARNER,
WALPOLE,	REYNOLDS,	MONTAGUE,
		&c. &c.

To which are added, NOTES by
SAMUEL JOHNSON and GEORGE STEEVENS;
Together with
THE PREFACES OF FORMER EDITORS:
TWO PORTRAITS OF THE AUTHOR;
A FAC-SIMILE OF HIS HAND-WRITING;

A Plate, representing the Figures of ancient Morris-Dancers, &c. &c.
The Second Edition, revised and augmented.

—Τῆς φύσεως γραμματεὺς ἦν, τὸν κάλαμον ἀποβρέχων εἰς νῦν.
Vet. Auct. apud Suidam.

Multa dies variusque labor mutabilis ævi
Retulit in melius, multos alterna revisens
Lusit, et in solido rursus fortuna locavit, Virgil.

Printed for J. NICHOLS, T. EVANS, and the rest of the PROPRIETORS.

23. Advertisement for *The Plays of William Shakespeare*, ed. Samuel Johnson and George Steevens.

understandably inquiring whether he had either "advised, or sanctioned" it. Malone answered quickly, denying any involvement with the reprint and wondering with obvious irritation: "who are to be the buyers after all? No one who knows anything of the matter will rely on it." Mockingly, Malone ventriloquized what he anticipated would be the enthusiastic, though uninformed response to the facsimile from "the gentlemen of the town": "Ay, now we shall have the true thing and perfectly understand this great author, without being bewildered by the commentators."[77]

But Malone's derision ironically had it exactly right. The contradictory, if mutually celebratory, conceptions of Shakespeare on the eighteenth-century stage and in the editorial tradition equally threatened to lose Shakespeare's work in their very efforts to ensure its continued appeal to new audiences and readers. Confronted with both, one might well say with King Lear "here's [two] on 's are sophisticated," but the typeset facsimile was as close as the age would get to "the thing itself" (*King Lear*, 3.4.98–9) – the "the true thing," in Malone's sarcastic term – close enough, indeed, that booksellers quickly turned to the Wrights' edition for pages to fill out imperfect copies of the original. But for readers unable to afford an authentic first folio, even one with replacement parts, the facsimile allowed virtually unmediated access to a Shakespeare edition that at least claimed to have provided what the contemporary editors had failed to do: Shakespeare's plays with texts exactly "as he conceiu'd the[m]" and free of the "whirlpool" of commentary that called into question their absolute authority. If Shakespeare was now indeed "an Englishman's secular bible,"[78] here was an edition proudly sounding the *sola scriptura* theme, like that which had marked the Protestantism of the time of its writing.

When Keats sat down to "read *King Lear* once again," he did so in his copy of the 1807 Wright reprint.[79] Clearly he wanted to enjoy "the bitter-sweet of this Shakespearean fruit" genetically unmodified. But lest this all seem merely one more narrative of *Authenticity Triumphans*, it is worth recalling that 1807 also was the year in which Henrietta and Thomas Bowdler first published their *Family Shakespeare*. Notoriously, here Shakespeare's text once again gave way, this time under the pressure of nineteenth-century middle-class propriety. The religious language that had surrounded the project of restoring the genuine Shakespearean text now graced an edition in which it was carefully purged of "every thing that could give offense to the religious and virtuous mind."[80] Over thirty editions of the *Family Shakespeare* would be published before the end of the century; at least for a time, decency, rather than authenticity, would be the principle that would most powerfully determine the English enthusiasm for Shakespeare.

CHAPTER FOUR

From codex to computer; or, presence of mind

Books are ashamed of still being books.

Theodor W. Adorno

The first three chapters of this book represent my own efforts to engage with one of the most productive developments of recent Shakespeare scholarship: the exploration of the complex motivations and practices of the book trade that took Shakespeare's scripts, written to be performed, and turned them into books to be purchased and read, and in the process turned Shakespeare, through no effort of his own, from a playwright into an author, from a man of the theater to a man in print.[1] If the book was, however, not Shakespeare's intended medium, it was obviously one well known to him, as printed books were part of the vibrant cultural and commercial world of his London. Now Shakespeare has once again been thrust into a medium other than the one he chose for himself – the brave new world of electronic texts – but this one, of course, 'tis new to him, one he never even imagined.

It is indeed one that most of *us* never imagined, even as little as ten years ago. But it is a world we now inhabit, and a world in which Shakespeare lives – on hard disks, on CD-ROM, on the internet, on digital tapes, his words presented to us not in the impressions of inked type on paper but in the transient representations of encoded data strings translated into letter forms by our computers' central processing units.

Usually this fact is greeted with not much more than a yawn. In spite of some apocalyptic bluster in the air, we have already comfortably made the transition to the digital text, even if its actual technology remains unfathomable to most users. I wrote this chapter not with a pen on paper but on a computer (in fact on several, happily carrying my words on a disk back and forth between them). Even printed books are today more often than not produced and stored digitally. But this is not what generates either the dread or the euphoria of those contemplating the future of the book – or its lack of one. What they focus on is not the mode of production or storage but the delivery system. Digitally *produced* books are unmistakably still books; digitally *displayed* books are not.

Seemingly, then, what generates the strong emotions is not the technology enabling the writing of the text or its reproduction; what generates strong emotions is the form in which it is encountered. How the words got there does not seem to cause a problem; it is where "there" is that does. "There," in our digital age, is increasingly an electronic environment, the text existing only on a screen, or, more precisely and to the point, *not* existing but appearing on it, no longer a fixed but a fluid entity.

For the new technological utopians this is the very mark of digitization's virtue: it offers an escape from the felt tyranny of the book. The book, once brilliantly conceived by Elizabeth Eisenstein as "an agent of change,"[2] seems to many now a force of repression in the information age. The electronic text is readily conceived of as what one scholar has called a "liberation technology," the means, in Jay Bolter's phrase, "to free the writing from the frozen structure of the page."[3] Enthusiasts of the new technologies have adopted an emancipatory rhetoric in which information would be liberated from its material restraints. "Information wants to be free" is Stewart Brand's revolutionary cry.[4] (I am reminded of my favorite bit of graffiti from my days at the University of Chicago in the troubled summer of 1968: "Free the Bound Periodicals.") But the very exuberance of the utopian's embrace has predictably led other voices to answer with technological Jeremiads, promising woe to the people who bow to this false God and turn their backs upon what George Steiner calls "real presence."[5]

But the text displayed on a computer screen is no more or no less real than the text printed on paper. If by "real presence" one intends the inescapable materiality by which the text becomes available for reading, then the computer has no less a claim to it than the book; the digital text may be less sensually satisfying, but it is hard to see in what sense it can be thought any less "real." Or, if by "real presence" one means the authority of the creative intelligence that the written text reflects and reveals but that any materiality must betray, then neither the book nor the computer has a compelling claim to it. Both, of course, mediate the written word, though differently, and perhaps what is most disturbing about the utopian view of the new technology is not the threatened loss of whatever it is Steiner means by "real presence" but the unthinking ease with which it transfers the desire for freedom and autonomy from people to information.

Most of us, however, contemplate our existence in what has been called "the last days of the book"[6] with considerable equanimity. It might be, of course, that we have not quite grasped the enormous changes that await us, but it seems that our habits of reading have already changed in ways that seem unthreatening. We check our e-mail and surf the internet looking for information and things to buy. (It is probably worth observing, however, that, at least as I write this, more books are sold over the internet than any other consumer item.) If we are concerned with the loss of "presence" in the new medium, it is presence conceived of more as a somatic experience than as a mental one. We seem in these now familiar discussions more often to be worrying about the stimulation of nerve-endings than of brain synapses. "Words on the screen," said John Updike, "give the sense of being just another passing electronic wriggle," but the book has a satisfying physicality: "the charming little clothy box of the thing, the smell of the glue, even the print, which has its own beauty."[7] And beyond the aesthetic argument there is the argument of convenience; for all the ringing claims of hypertextual freedom, the electronic text is tied to an unwieldy container. Hence the familiar reservation that you cannot read an electronic text in the bath. As we rationalize our resistance to digitization, we reveal the fetishism of our relationship to the book. We are all too much like a toddler with a favorite, old blanket; the book comforts us because it feels good and we can carry it around.

I am always happy to be comforted, but both arguments for the superiority of the printed book seem weak ones, partially because they are too easily countered by a technology that will soon be able to reproduce in a digital form, if it has not already done so, the physical experience of the book. The e-book is already here, and there is no technological reason why it cannot approximate "the charming little clothy box" that Updike savors; and if it probably will still not be a good idea to take an e-book with you in the bath, neither is taking any conventionally printed book that you really value. (Indeed we should remember how late in the history of the printed book came the portability and the sheer banality of the object that allowed a reader to take it into the tub.) Consider this recent magazine review of an e-book: "sufficiently svelte to be read comfortably with one hand, its screen backlit a soothing bluish-white, the RocketBook may save several marriages while drying up the market for clip-on lights."[8] At the very least this reminds us that new technologies are no less liable to be fetishized than the old ones, but it also makes clear how soon the physical disadvantages of the electronic environment will be overcome.

The real reason, however, that the arguments about comfort seem weak is that, however true they may be, they are almost certainly displacements of a still deeper discomfort, not so much with the environment of the electronic text but with the electronic text itself. The relative fixity of ink on paper gives way to the fluidity of pixels on a screen. All the previous technologies of writing involved more or less permanently marking the environment; cutting, brushing, pressing words into a medium chosen to receive and preserve them. Electronic texts work differently, both technologically and ontologically; their elements of meaning are "fundamentally unstable."[9]

I type a word and it appears on a screen, but my action on the keyboard does not cause the word to appear there in the direct fashion that it did when I typed on a typewriter. With a typewriter, striking the key drove a metal rod tipped with a piece of appropriately cut metal first against an inked ribbon and then further forward, pressing the ribbon, now distended by the letter shape, against a piece of paper fixed between the ribbon and a cylindrical roller; as the rod fell back, an inked impression of the letter was left on the paper. The letter then existed for as long as the paper survived or until the ink faded (and even then the letter form indistinctly remained in the paper, as its fibers were compromised when they were struck by the type). On the computer keyboard, striking the letter sends an electronic impulse to the computer, which translates it into a binary code and stores it in this form in its memory; it then sends a string of coded instructions to the monitor, stimulating a set of cells to form patterns of light and dark spaces that produce an image of the letter on the screen. When the electronic impulse from computer to monitor is cut off, the letter disappears, leaving on the screen no trace that it was ever there.

It can, of course, be recovered. If I have "saved" what I have typed (and to "save" is merely to move the coded instruction to an environment in which an electronic impulse is not necessary to maintain it), I can send a new instruction to return what has been saved to the screen. But, of course, what was there before is not what reappears. Calling up the saved text does not actually retrieve what was previously present but, rather, reconstitutes the data stream, enabling it to be reproduced. As Michael Joyce says, "Print stays itself, electronic text replaces itself."[10]

It seems to me that it is actually this ontological distinction between the electronic text and the printed text that unsettles, which if true means that the mode of production is, in fact, every bit as much the issue as the mode of display. Texts in this form are fluid and transient, clearly separate from the physical instantiations that enable them to be read. "The reader always encounters a virtual image of a stored text," in George Landow's words, "and not the original version itself."[11]

But this may reveal what is finally so unnerving about electronic texts. The one thing the new technology makes abundantly clear is that texts are never self-sufficient but demand mediation to become available for reading. This, however, is not unique to digitization. One could say as well of any printed book that it is a virtual image of a text (assuming that "'virtual" does not merely mean, as it threatens to, computer generated) and not the original version itself. Over the last 500 years, however, the technology of the book has become so seemingly inevitable that we fail to see it as a mediation. It seems to contain the text as naturally as skin on a human body. We have to remind ourselves, as Roger Stoddard has tried to do, that whatever it is that authors do, they do not write books;[12] the seemingly counter-intuitive claim is obvious once one thinks of the difference in the material relation of painters to their paintings and authors to the books that bear their names. What is perhaps most unnerving about electronic texts, then, is not merely that they are virtual but that they are no more virtual than any other text we read.

In this moment – and it will be just a moment – of unfamiliarity and unease, the electronic text serves to focus our attention upon the nature of what it is we read, not the content but the container. Soon the new medium will be as unavoidable, and thus as invisible, as the one it is, if not replacing, at least competing with as the dominant environment for the written word. But for now it conspicuously foregrounds the material make-up of the text, precisely by the novelty and, for most of us, the daunting unintelligibility of the medium. The electronic text makes us think about what we might call the physical predicament of the text in a way the book stopped doing for readers sometime in the sixteenth century. "To read a book" has for hundreds of years meant exactly the same thing as to read the text that the book materializes, the distinction itself seemingly a graceless and unnecessary scholasticism. But the book no more coincides with the text it embodies than does the computer that stores and delivers the digital text. It is no more its natural or inevitable environment.

Not least of the unnaturalnesses of the book is its self-containment, its physical assertion of the autonomy and coherence of the text. The covers that embrace it seemingly seal it off from its own complex historicity, deliver it ostensibly whole and uncontaminated to act upon its readers. "The covers of a book are responsible for much error," wrote T. E. Hulme well before there was an obvious alternative to them. "They set a limit around certain convenient groups of ideas, when there are really no limits."[13] Electronic texts resist the "error" of the book's apparent integrity, their digitization making a different claim about the character of the text they embody. They expose it as provisional and porous, the unfamiliar materiality itself enacting the networks of dependency that literary theorists and historians of the book have almost simultaneously discovered as the very conditions of authorship that the book demands for its realization but that its physical presence would occlude.[14]

The electronic medium is still unnervingly visible to us, raising questions about the relation of the linguistic structures of the literary work to the material forms that make it available to be engaged, questions that are fundamental to literary studies. What is the relation between the text's formal and its material principles of causality? Do texts exist independently of the medium in which they appear, its material forms accidental and merely vehicular; or do they exist only in those forms, each a unique textual incarnation whose materiality itself crucially shapes meaning, altering in some way the significance of the linguistic organization of the work?

But, of course, the advent of the electronic medium did not force those questions on us. They were always there to be asked about the texts we read.[15] What, however, it has done in this regard is to make such questioning more likely, or, at very least, to make the avoidance of such questions less easy, as it denaturalizes our relation to the written word, making the fact of its problematic embodiment unmistakable. Once we seriously pose the questions the electronic medium has foregrounded for us, we find ourselves at the heart of the issues that animate contemporary textual theory.[16] Indeed the choice between thinking of the text as essentially independent of its medium and seeing the text as the product of it defines the two major positions in the current debate, and a short detour to explore them may well clarify what the electronic text both demands of and offers us, as the environment of our reading increasingly moves "from book to screen."[17]

One strand of the discussion reflects what might be thought a platonic tradition, whose most compelling contemporary voice is G. Thomas Tanselle, who insists that a "work is not fully knowable through any of its written manifestations," the surviving documents (in Tanselle's vocabulary) always being "imperfect guides to the work they attempt to transmit." Indeed Tanselle's idealist concept of "the work" leads him to maintain that it "cannot exist in physical form."[18] The other is what can be called a pragmatic tradition, represented most influentially by Jerome McGann, who, not insignificantly, was among the first textual scholars actively to explore the possibilities of electronic texts, and who argues that the distinction between the immaterial work and the various texts of it that exist in material form, however useful analytically, is unsustainable except theoretically, since what Tanselle thinks of as "the work" is unknowable except as it is manifested in some physical form. "Literary works do not know themselves, and cannot be known," writes McGann, "apart from their specific material modes of existence/resistance."[19]

Traditionally, "the duty of an editor," as R. B. McKerrow wrote, has been understood as the effort "merely to present those works as he believes the author to have intended them to appear," rather than to present any of their surviving texts.[20] If McKerrow's "merely" hides a whole set of problematic assumptions about the task of editing (no less than his unselfconscious masculine pronoun does about those who edit), modern editors (female and male) usually have set out to recover the author's intended words from the inevitable distortions of the printed record, to return them to their pristine condition "before," as Dover Wilson revealingly wrote, "they became defiled with printer's ink."[21] Especially with Shakespeare, whose plays were published with no interest or involvement on his part, editors try to retrieve his unmediated intentions from the confusing testimony of the early printed texts. "*The aim of a critical edition*," as Greg said in his first "rule" for editors, "*should be to present the text, so far as the available evidence permits, in the form in which we may suppose that it would have stood in fair copy, made by the author himself, of the work as he finally intended it.*"[22] The editors work to "strip the veil of print from the text," in Fredson Bowers's famous phrase,[23] in order to discover the author's intended text that has been betrayed by the material forms in which it circulated. In the printing house the work inevitably was altered – by the desires of publishers, by the practices of compositors and printers, as well as by the imperfections and limitations of the medium itself; and editors, by carefully considering the surviving textual witnesses, along with the author's verbal habits, orthographic practices, and the procedures of the printing house, are often able to speculate with some confidence on what an author actually wrote, which either never reached print or which did, but has become so tangled in non-authorial variants that the authentic reading is no longer self-evident.

Since the goal of critical editing so understood is the recovery of the intended work from its material circumstances, the resulting, edited text has no necessary relation to any medium in which it can be presented. The motivating principle of such editing is precisely that the medium is at very best a neutral conveyor of the intended work and more likely a detrimental environment, disbursing authority to agents other than the author and obscuring or defiling the "ideal text" of the author's imagining. If the medium is understood primarily as vehicular, the necessary choice of one text (or more) for the critical edition itself must, therefore, be a function of considerations external to it. A critical edition could be published as easily in an electronic form as in a printed book; whatever advantage one might have over the other is clearly independent of the internal logic of the edition itself.

Yet whatever physical form the critical edition takes, its fundamental commitment to authorial intention becomes problematic in the case of drama. How appropriate is it for a playwright's intentions to be the object of editorial desire purposefully isolated from their role within the necessarily collective energies of the theater? All writers write within a set of enabling (and sometimes inhibiting) imaginative and institutional conditions, but the playwright alone works in circumstances that are radically collaborative, which indeed are designed to subordinate individual literary ambitions to a communal artistic achievement. A playwright's writings are, as Auden almost said, always modified in the guts of the living theater, subjected to rearrangements, cuts, and interpolations by the demands of performance. The authorial text, even if it can be recovered, is then only that – an authorial text, which can never be thought identical to the play. (And the irony should be noted that a bibliographic theory developed to rescue authorial intentions from their material compromise came from scholars interested primarily in Shakespeare and other Renaissance playwrights.)

But it is not obvious, in any case, that the authorial text *can* be recovered from the deforming print record. Certainly some types of textual deficiency are easily recognized and remedied – a turned letter, for example, or an obvious mis-spelling – but in other cases even the putative deficiency is usually a matter of critical judgment rather than bibliographic fact. Pope found the metrical irregularity of Shakespeare's verse evidence not of Shakespeare's deliberate artistry but of textual corruption and "corrected" it, corrections that in many cases are still present in modern editions.

The commitment to an ideal text that lies obscurely behind what has been printed is not easily abandoned.

Even today editors often emend where their own sense of the work's intrinsic perfection seemingly demands it. Stanley Wells, for example, has argued that "we should pay our poet the compliment of assuming that he cares for metrical values, and be willing to emend when the surviving text is demonstrably deficient."[24] One might object, however, that this brings us disturbingly close to the intrusive practices of Pope, insisting on metrical norms that "our poet" – and Wells's *autonomasia* is revealing – could easily have chosen to violate, and forcing us to invent and insert various expletive syllables to regularize a line.

But even at an obviously more contestable verbal level, the same tendencies can be discovered. For example, in Gary Taylor's Oxford *Henry V* (1984), the King feels that none of his remorse for his father's usurpation of Richard's crown is effectual, "Since that my penitence comes after ill, / Imploring pardon" (4.1.292–3); although in the folio (the only source for these lines) Henry's penitence comes not "after *ill*" but "after *all*" (emphases mine). For Taylor the emendation is required because the "all" of the folio is unclear and, as such, it "would amount to a major artistic flaw" (p. 298); and so it must be fixed. "As emended," Taylor concludes contentedly, "the passage provides exactly the right balance between a pious Henry, aware like every true Christian of the inadequacy of his own or any man's penitence, and the audience's knowledge of the coming victory at Agincourt, which is a proof that God in fact does not hold Henry responsible for his father's sin, and has accepted his efforts at atonement and his plea for pardon" (p. 301).

Taylor's confidence that the emendation provides "exactly the right balance" becomes possible only with an *a priori* sense of the intentions of the author. Though the emendation is graphically plausible, presupposing only a compositorial confusion of "a" and "i", it is clearly determined by critical rather than bibliographic considerations: the commitment not to allow Shakespeare to be guilty of "a major artistic flaw" (though on precisely such critical grounds one might argue that Taylor's "ill" leaves Shakespeare guilty of at least a minor *logical* flaw, since penitence that did not come "after ill" would be pointless) and the conviction that

Shakespeare intended in the speech to achieve "exactly the right balance" between Henry's awareness of his imperfections and an audience's reluctance to see them. This is not to denigrate Taylor's editorial achievements; he is perhaps the most brilliant of our textual scholars. It is only to show that interpretation is unmistakably as much productive of texts as it is responsive to them.

In spite of our obvious yearning for the "real presence" of Shakespeare lurking behind his damaged texts, and our willingness to act at least on occasion as if we have found it, what we have are only the printed texts, which in various ways no doubt distort Shakespeare's intentions. But they are all we have. In the absence of any holograph manuscripts, which, even were one to surface, would still provide us with less certainty about Shakespeare's intentions than we imagine,[25] the early printed texts are usually as close as we can get to Shakespeare's writing. The camera's loving close-ups of Joseph Feinnes' ink-stained fingers in *Shakespeare in Love* eloquently speak our continuing desire for presence, but only seven signatures on various documents and perhaps the 146 lines in the manuscript of *Sir Thomas More* survive to give actual evidence of Shakespeare's hand.

I am not suggesting that authorial intentions are unimportant, only that in Shakespeare's case they are unavailable, and in every case they are never solely determining of the play either as it is performed or printed. But I do believe they matter. Authors have intentions, and to some degree they are recoverable, though probably only to the degree that the published text successfully represents them; but no book ever appears that fully and only expresses these. An author's intentions are realizable only as they interact with the intentions of other agents. The process of book production, no less than the process of play production, distributes an author's intentions through the material and institutional conditions of production. Even Blake's singular efforts to control all aspects of the production process finally found their limits in the materiality of the medium itself.

If, then, an author's intentions are not fully represented in or responsible for the printed book, the editorial commitment to their recovery might be recognized as quixotic – since the very condition that makes editing necessary, the absence of an authoritative text, means that at most what can be claimed for the edited text is that it is a plausible reconstruction of the authorially intended text, a text that never physically existed prior to the completion of the editorial labor. And such a commitment must be also seen as tendentious – since the very commitment to the reconstruction of the authorial text is ideological (I mean this literally not judgmentally) rather than inevitable, a reasonable but by no means necessary grant of authority to the intended text over the actual textual forms in which it is encountered. Neither of these are reasons *not* to edit with the aim of reconstructing the author's intended text – the author's intentions are of course a worthy, if elusive, object of study – though both are reasons to recognize that there must be alternative ways to conceive of the goals of editorial activity, ways in which the processes of materialization would not be understood as unwanted obstacles to the realization of the author's intention but as the necessary conditions of it.

If what we want to read is that which would exist if the writing had not been subjected to what Tanselle calls "the hazards of the physical" (*Rationale*, p. 93), then the conventional understanding and practices of editing are appropriate: at least the text so conceived is the object they would reconstruct, and the procedures that have been developed are suitably designed for and have often brilliantly been deployed in its reconstruction. An ideal text ("ideal" in the sense that it represents the work of the author's imagining before it has suffered the various intrusive processes of its materialization) can be more or less successfully reconstructed and presented to view. If, however, our interest is not in the unrealized and probably unrealizable intended text but in the physical manifestations of it that, even in (or, rather, precisely in) their imperfection, testify to the actual conditions of historical existence, then the editorial task and challenge is different.

Once one takes as one's goal not the isolation of authorial intentions from their enabling forms and circumstances but precisely the opposite – the location of the text within the network of social and institutional practices that have allowed it to be produced and read – it becomes more difficult to imagine the form such an edition would assume and the procedures by which one would edit. Indeed arguably it becomes more difficult to justify editing at all, since the unedited texts, even in their manifest error, are the most compelling witnesses to the complex conditions of their production. Editing can only obscure or distort some of the evidence provided by those early texts, erasing marks of the texts' historicity.[26]

There are, of course, good reasons for editions, in fact for many kinds of editions, though probably not very good reasons for as many of the same kinds of editions as indeed we have. Shakespeare should be available in editions that do attempt to restore the play he wrote before it was subjected to the demands of production in both the playhouse and the printing house; but he should also be available in editions that take the theatrical auspices of the plays seriously, recognizing that primary among Shakespeare's intentions was the desire to write something that could be successfully played. Both of these texts should be available in modernized spelling, in cheap paperbacks of individual plays and in collections of the complete works, as well as in edited old-spelling editions. And Shakespeare should be available unedited, in facsimiles of the early printings. But even a facsimile can never reveal all the material information carried by the early text – for example, the paper quality – and, what even more limits its value, facsimile makes normative a single copy of a text that almost certainly would differ in various ways from every other copy in the print run. (And therefore even an original playbook would not perfectly represent the play, though it would be very nice to have.) Each of these different texts would offer something to the reader of Shakespeare that the others do not, and each of course has fundamental limitations, denying the reader information of one sort or another that is elsewhere available and in certain circumstances would be consequential.

The Shakespeare section of the bookshop ideally might stock examples of each of these, but in truth, though we can usually find several editions of a single play (at least if the play is *Hamlet* or *King Lear*; if it is *King John* or *Pericles* we might not be able to find even one), the several editions are all too much alike, the text in modernized spelling with more or less annotation depending on whether it is intended for a scholastic market, for universities, or for the general reader. Marketing considerations rather than intellectual ones have largely determined what we can find on bookshop shelves, and marketing considerations have in large part dictated a wasteful duplication of scholarly energy and a conscious neglect of other kinds of texts that might genuinely be of value. I am not blaming publishers for this situation; book publishing is expensive, and publishers today, no less than the publishers of the early texts of Shakespeare's plays, need to feel confident that there will be some return on their investment. Still it is not clear to me, for example, that there is not at least a small profit to be made by a publisher from an affordable, paperback series that – unlike the New Cambridge, New Penguin, Oxford, Arden, or even, ironically, Harvester's "Shakespearean Originals" – would present the texts in facsimiles of their first appearance in print.

But, in any case, if one wished to see the text in its full historical materiality no one of the various kinds of texts would serve. A scholar would inevitably want them all – and more: all the early printings; the restoration redactions, which were, of course, the form in which many of the plays were seen for almost 150 years; the often brilliant if quirky eighteenth-century editions beginning with Rowe's; the Globe text of the 1860s, the form in which Shakespeare first circumnavigated the world; the various important modern editions. We know that the play is not fully represented in any one edition, in spite of the overt or implicit claims it might make to being definitive. The impressive paratextual assertions of an edition's authority – the imposing introductions, the heavy annotations, the lengthy, if usually unintelligible, collation notes – all of which exist to assert the editor's control over the text, testify at least as eloquently to the text's resistant instabilities as to the editor's success in resolving them.

In truth, as this book is in part designed to show, Shakespeare's texts remain unnervingly (exhilaratingly?) fluid in spite of over 375 years of editorial efforts to stabilize them. In the absence of an authentic original, indeed in the absence of a general agreement about what an authentic original might be, each edition, like each performance, of a play becomes part of a cumulative history of what has been experienced as the play; and the more of this history that is available the more it becomes possible to measure the play's achievement and its effects. The individual print edition, however, almost always has to think otherwise about the text; it usually must choose a single instantiation, a choice usually driven less by editorial confidence than by inescapable considerations of space, of cost, of readability, all exposing the limits of the codex as a tool of information technology.

But this brings us explicitly back to the topic with which we began, for the advent of electronic texts perhaps offers an escape from, if not a resolution of, the struggle between incompatible textual understandings and preferences. The capaciousness of the electronic environment seemingly allows an edition in this new medium to offer any number of textual versions, both the edited text of the work and any or all of the texts of the documents that previously have represented it.[27]

The fact that the electronic text does not reside on the screen on which we read it, unlike the printed text, which obviously does physically inhabit the page on which it is read, allows it a freedom from the material limits that define the book. Size is no longer a necessary consideration of textual production; the text is apparently not bound by concerns about convenience or cost. Indeed, literally the text is not bound at all.

And with that material freedom comes another. The electronic text is permeable in a way the printed text is not, not isolated from other texts in its physical integrity but existing in the same environment, so that, indeed, it is unable to "shut out other texts" that are networked with it.[28] Any document can be linked to and thus become part of any other text. The resulting hypertext is thus the materialization of a Barthian conception of textuality itself, a textual environment in which any text can intersect and be intersected by an infinite number of others.[29] And every work within it can itself be multiply realized, available both in discrete and conflated versions, prepared according to any number of assumptions and principles; instead of an ideal(ized) text, we have the text explicitly as polymorph, its multiplicity organized as what George Landow calls "a complex field of variants" (*Hypertext*, p. 56) rather than as a collection (or collation) of deviations from some imagined perfection.

The possibilities for editorial practice are obvious.[30] A full consideration of the possibilities for *writing itself* in hypertext (rather than what I am concerned with here: the hypertext *edition*) is well beyond the scope of this essay, indeed well beyond the scope of this

Virtual Reading Room
Columbia Text Workbench

Work: Shakespeare, *King Lear*

Texts	*Reference*
original	indexes
variants	encyclopedias
translations	dictionaries
other works of author	maps /atlases
other works of corpus	commentaries
works beyond corpus	bibliographies

Searching	*Extra-textual*
words	audio
phrases	video
formal features	art
combinations	music

Columbia: libraries   syllabi   notepads

SEARCH: realm or kingdom in *Lear* (re:5.3)
Rule in this realm, and the gored state sustain
Rule in this kingdom, and the good state sustain

Search results for "realm" in *Lear*–1 other
3.2:Then shall the realm of Albion
[Pelican 3.2.91 FOOL]
Search results for "kingdom" in *Lear*–12 others
1.1:division of the kingdom, it appears not
1.1:In three our kingdom: and 'tis our fast intent
1.1:Remain this ample third of our fair kingdom
1.1:Upon our kingdom: if, on the tenth day
   following
2.1:I will send far and near, that all the kingdom
2.4:Thy half o' the kingdom hast thou not forgot
3.1:Into this scatter'd kingdom; who already
3.2:I never gave you kingdom, call'd you
   children
3.7:Late footed in the kingdom
4.3:of; which imports to the kingdom so much
4.7:In your own kingdom, sir
4.7:powers of the kingdom approach apace

Shakespeare, *King Lear* 5.3 [Pelican]   previous   next

ALBANY
Bear them from hence. Our present business
Is general woe.
   [To Kent and Edgar] Friends of my soul, you twain
Rule in this realm, and the gored state sustain.

KENT
I have a journey, sir, shortly to go.
My master calls me; I must not say no.

EDGAR
The weight of this sad time we must obey;
Speak what we feel, not what we ought to say.
The oldest hath borne most; we that are young
Shall never see so much, nor live so long.
                    Exeunt with a dead march

Shakespeare, *Lear* 5.3 [1619 Quarto]   previous   next

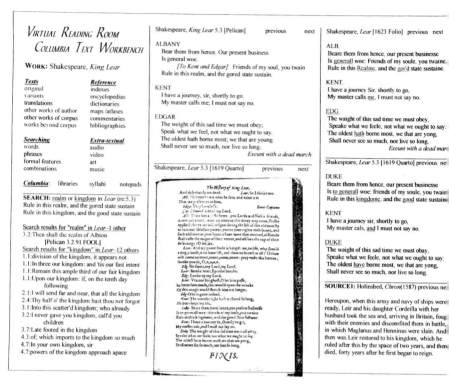

Shakespeare, *Lear* [1623 Folio] previous next

ALB.
Beare them from hence, our present businesse
Is generall woe: Friends of my soule, you twaine.
Rule in this Realme, and the gor'd state sustaine.

KENT.
I have a journey Sir, shortly to go,
My master calls me, I must not say no.

EDG.
The waight of this sad time we must obey,
   Speake what we feele, not what we ought to say:
The oldest hath borne most, we that are young,
Shall never see so much, nor live so long.

Shakespeare, *Lear* 5.3 [1619 Quarto] previous ne

DUKE
Beare them from hence, our present businesse
Is to generall woe: friends of my soule, you twain
Rule in this kingdome, and the good state sustain

KENT
I have a journey sir, shortly to go.

DUKE
The waight of this sad time we must obay,
Speake what we feele, not what we ought to say:
The oldest have borne most, we that are yong,
Shall never see so much, nor live so long.

SOURCE1: Holinshed, *Chron*(1587) previous ne

Hereupon, when this army and navy of ships were
ready, Leir and his daughter Cordeilla with her
husband took the sea and, arriving in Britain, foug
with their enemies and discomfited them in battle,
in which Maglanus and Henninus were slain. And
then was Leir restored to his kingdom, which he
ruled after this by the space of two years, and then
died, forty years after he first began to reign.

24. Hypertext page, *"King Lear"* (Columbia University, Literature/Humanities)

writer. Nonetheless, it may be useful to observe that most of the discussions of writing in the electronic environment emphasize the reader's activity in constructing the text, exploiting the nature of the medium itself, which allows the reader endlessly and effortlessly to reshape the elements it contains. "Electronic technology," as Bolter says, "makes texts particular and individual" (*Writing Space*, p. 9). The electronic edition, however, offers the reader a different kind of freedom: not to restructure the elements themselves, but to engage them in ways that may well be "particular and individual" as the reader navigates (but leaves unchanged) the materials available. But it is precisely the potential copiousness of what is there is to navigate that seems to suggest a way out of the disabling binaries of recent editorial theory.

In the past, regardless of the particular textual history of the work to be edited or the individual editor's understanding of the activity of editing itself, the nature of the codex exerts itself upon the task, helping to determine the form of the edition. Externally imposed limits of size and cost normally dictated the need to select (or construct) a single version of the work. But such contingencies no longer force an editor to choose between versions, because in hypertext there is no physical limit to the number of textual manifestations that can appear. All "variants and variations," as Patrick Conner has written, "can be present and linked as nodes, and even processed into the text, so that one can reproduce any version of the text one wishes,"[31] even versions which have had no material existence, like the ideal text of the author's – or an editor's – imagination. For a Shakespeare edition, one could have an edited text (or indeed more than one), as well as digital facsimiles of all early printings; and additional resources could be included, like source texts or concordances, theater reviews, illustrations, audio clips, and even film versions, all of which can be linked to allow easy movement back and forth between them.

But this will come as no surprise. In writing this I feel something like Milton's Abdiel, who "found / Already known what he for news had thought / to have reported" (*Paradise Lost*, VI, 19–21). Such hypertextual resources already exist and are increasingly familiar. Figure 24 is an example of a characteristic hypertext screen. This was produced with resources readily available in the

Columbia library by a friend, Richard Sacks, for Columbia's version of a great books course, known familiarly as Lit./Hum. Done with more time and access to other materials it could, of course, be improved (among other things, I would not have used the 1619 *Lear* quarto – one of those texts that was intended for the aborted collection that Pavier and Jaggard had planned,[32] but rather Butter's 1608 Q1). But the extraordinary possibilities of hypertext should be clear even from the picture. On the left there is a menu of options; on the top a clean, modernized text, familiar in its typography and textual detail; below that the related page scanned from an early text (and in principle one could have any number of early and edited texts correlated to what serves as the organizing, control text). On the right are folio and quarto texts in modern typography with variants highlighted. In the bottom right is the relevant source material from Holinshed; in the bottom left, a word search that might clarify the potentially interesting implications of one of these variants: the folio's "Realme" and the quarto's "kingdome," in Albany's offer to Kent and Edgar "you twaine / Rule in this Realme" or "Rule in this Kingdome."

Among the most impressive of the existing electronic editions of Shakespeare is the project developed by Peter Donaldson at MIT, called (somewhat less imaginatively than most new electronic endeavours) "The Shakespeare Electronic Archive." To give a sense of its extraordinary capacity, the archived *Hamlet* includes, in addition to an electronic text derived from the Oxford *Complete Works*, "high resolution facsimiles of all pages of the First Folio in both corrected and uncorrected states, complete facsimiles of all individual copies of both *Hamlet* quartos, 1,500 works of *Hamlet* art and illustration, and several *Hamlet* films."[33] All this material is easily accessible, and most of it is linked to the base text so a user can click on a bit of text and access a menu of the bibliographic and performative options that define that particular segment of the play.

The *Hamlet* project – and other such undertakings – either ends the need for editing or, more likely, re-establishes it. If such resources, in their ability to offer a density of relevant material that no print edition could ever manage, perhaps suggest that we are now free from the traditional obligation of textual editing to produce versions of the plays as "their author intended them to appear," that very density may itself reinaugurate the desire for a single text that the electronic archive has seemingly rendered both inadequate and unnecessary. No doubt such hypertextual resources could be used to confirm the truth of Wittgenstein's dictum that "only the exhaustive is interesting,"[34] but, in their "exhaustive" and exhausting copiousness, they may make the play (choosing my words carefully) virtually unreadable.

But the MIT project is not an edition; it is not designed to be read. It is an archive, and like any archive it yields its treasures only to diligent and capable researchers. An edition, however, is designed to present not the archive but the results of one's investigations there. If such results can be no more authoritative than the completeness of the archive and the competence of the investigator permit, they can, within those limits, present a text that can confidently and conveniently be read – not perhaps as Shakespeare's *Hamlet*, for what in truth can that mean, but as Harold Jenkins' *Hamlet*, or G. R. Hibbard's *Hamlet*, or, soon, as Ann Thompson and Neil Taylor's *Hamlet*, the editorial priority not an arrogation of creative authority but a frank admission of the edition's inevitable idiosyncrasies and limitations.

Usually, of course, these are hardly disabling. (Sometimes, however, they are: a recent edition of *Hamlet* did appear with the Prince musing, "To be or to be," the terrifying absence of real choice, I take it, clearly the cause of his tragedy.) For the general reader, for most students, for actors, the various, competent editions in print serve them well. They all want to read the play, not reconstruct it, and if what in fact they read is a version edited according to any one of the several plausible understandings of what the play is, it is an acceptable compromise. For most purposes what we want is just the play, responsibly edited, clearly presented, inexpensive, and sufficiently well manufactured that the pages do not fall out once the book has been opened.

For the scholar, however, that phrase "just the play" is the vexing issue. What is *just* the play? The play on stage? What stage? What production? What night (or day)? The play as written? As the author first imagined it? Or after it was revised in the light of what was learned in performance? The *textus receptus*: the play as it has lived in history (for example, the editorially conflated text of *King Lear*, which at very least must be recognized as the primary form of the play that was read and acted for the last 150 years)? Which of these is "just the play"? Which of these is not?

The familiar dichotomy of the play on the page and the play on the stage gives way to another: the play on the printed page and the play on the computer screen. On the page, the play is stabilized, by print and by editorial commitment: a commitment to the author's final intention, to the surviving best text, to the performance text of a particular production, or, as often as not, merely to the text that is out of copyright and can be reprinted without cost. The codex is always about choices and boundaries; that is both its advantage and its limitation. On the screen, the play is always potentially multiple and unstable. There is no necessity to choose between textual understandings: all available versions of the play can theoretically be included, and we can move easily between them. That is both the advantage and the limitation of the electronic text.[35] The book disciplines; it makes us take responsibility for our decisions and live with their consequences. The electronic text offers a fantasy of freedom: there is no need make choices; there are no consequences to accept.

The book's reassuring offer of closure and authority gives way to the electronic text's exhilarating promise of possibility and an immunity from all restraint. It is, however, worth pausing to disrupt this neat binary by noting that its claim is only conceptually true. The book in fact is no more complete and closed than is the electronic text open and free. The integrity of books (as opposed to that of "the book," which is an ideological construct) is always vulnerable to the productive, and often perverse, reading habits of individuals, who are usually happy to mark, deface, copy, misread, or otherwise appropriate the books (or parts of books) they "read"; and, the apparent freedom of the electronic text is undermined by the not-inconsiderable costs of hardware, rights, data entry, site design and maintenance (to say nothing of the obvious difficulty of persuading anyone to pay for access, leading a number of electronic publishing ventures recently to be abandoned and others to be reconceived by their administrators as loss leaders), as well as the fact that, as electronic texts are dependent upon technologies that a reader does not own, the reader has distressingly little control over them. That is, Columbia University cannot remove a book that I own from my bookshelf, but it can easily remove the electronic version from a website that it maintains and that I have bookmarked for future access. (Do check the bookmarks in your web browser's address book and see how many can no longer be found.) The issue of how long sites will be maintained, like the related issue of how compatible the always improving technologies will be with the ones they render obsolete, is an important one for thinking about the electronic environment as an alternative to so-called "hard copy." (How many of the essays that any of us wrote on computers in the late 1980s and early 1990s are accessible even to their authors except as printed copies on paper?)

But even with these caveats in mind, the electronic text seduc-tively beckons, leading enthusiasts to trumpet the end of the age of print, and skeptics to murmur defensively that the book's longev-ity may have been underestimated. The printed book and the elec-tronic text come to define less alternative ways of engaging the word than alternative ways of engaging the world. One might easily escape the binary these alternatives pose by saying what is no doubt true – but also no doubt uninteresting – that they both have a useful role to play, the alternatives in fact offering themselves less as an ethical choice than what might be thought an erotic one. It is not which is good, or good for us, but which we desire or can con-vince ourselves (or our libraries) that we need.

More interesting to me, however, is why that escape is so easy. And it is easy, anyhow, as long as we think of print and electronic texts merely as tools. Sometimes you need a shovel, sometimes a rake, and there is no reason to think one better than another except in terms of its suitability for the specific job that needs doing. But if we pose the issue somewhat differently and think of them not as tools but as technologies, the ecumenical response begins to seem facile or naive. A technology, unlike a tool, is not merely a device with a particular function, but an ensemble of motives and means with institutional supports and cultural consequences. Its particu-lar instrumentality aside, the almost irresistible logic – or is it promise – of technological advance leads us to reject models of co-existence for models of replacement. "This will kill that" (*Ceci tuera cela*), famously says Hugo's archdeacon in *The Hunchback of Notre Dame*, holding a book and looking up at his Cathedral (a textual moment now almost *de rigueur* for futurists attempting to limn the digital future).[36]

Often, of course, some new "this" does successfully kill off some old "that." Only theater historians, for example, remember what it literally means to be "in the limelight." But, not uncommonly, the old technologies prove far more vigorous than we might have thought. Painting survived photography, the movies survived television, and manuscript has survived print – though in each case technological enthusiasts confidently embraced the new and assured anyone who would listen that "this will kill that." Even the typewriter still survives (though barely) as the only means in many cases to fill out printed forms. Is the book, then, the "limelight" of information, destined to be recalled in the future only in a metaphor whose actual referent will be forgotten; or is the book, like painting, an unusually resilient mode of human communication that future generations will ingeniously adapt to their own needs and desires?

Of course, I do not know. No one does. The book will survive if the habits of reading that it not only supported but indeed established survive as well. If I had to bet, I would say that the book will survive in recognizable forms for many years (and that not the least of the achievements of the new age of electronic texts will prove to be that it forces us to recognize the book itself as a technology with its own considerable advantages), but would also predict that the existing systems of book publication and distribution will radically and quickly change. The real answer, however, will only come clear in time and will depend on a more searching test of the book's cultural logic than it has had to undergo since it first displaced the culture of the manuscript. Faced with the challenge from a digital technology that is unquestionably more capacious, more flexible, and more easily disseminated than print, can the book's self-confident offer of coherence and authority continue to compel?

Perhaps here the example of the Shakespeare edition can help clarify the issues. In some obvious way, hypertextual versions of a play offer a richer, more textured conception of what a particular play is than any print version could ever do. John Lavagnino has, however, claimed that, in spite of the usefulness of the material such hypertext archives might present, they inevitably are of limited value "because they don't go beyond *utility* to the attempt to change our *understanding* of those texts."[37] But it seems to me that precisely the reason they are valuable is that they do change that understanding. It is not merely that hypertext expands the capacities of the traditional print edition, including a greater number of textual versions and allowing these to be linked to a dense network of contextual information; it is that hypertext models a different conception of the play altogether, arguably one truer to its nature in that the hypertextual edition acknowledges in its very structure that the play is fundamentally something less stable and coherent than the printed edition necessarily represents it as being.

There is not a single text that is *Hamlet*, not only because it exists in three, different early printed texts, but because it exists also in all the performances of the play, each of course different, even in the same production-run, all the different films, different editions, even different translations. *Hamlet* is perhaps best considered not something in itself at all but, rather, the name for what allows us comfortably to consider as some metaphysical unity the various instantiations of the play; *Hamlet* is the name, that is, not for some pre-representational original but for something like what Gregory Bateson calls "the pattern that connects."[38] Even a hypertext version, however, could not include literally all that it "connects" – at very least the theatrical performances can not be fully recovered – but a hypertext *Hamlet* tells us that the play is not identical with a single text of the play. The variant texts, images, audio, and film, so easily linked and navigated in hypertext, are not, then, supplementary materials but are primary evidence of the play's fundamental existence as something multiple and variable.

In a print edition, however, a play becomes singular and fixed. Even those early printings, offering the play "as it was diuerse times publicly acted," still offer a single text, no doubt different from what indeed was spoken on any of the diverse occasions of its playing. In print, the play absorbs from the book in which it appears qualities foreign to its own nature. The physical integrity of the book at once carries and imposes a set of cultural assumptions independent of the particular printed text. It closes off and secures the text, offers it as complete and comprehensible in itself, and assigns it to its author as the guarantor of its originality. We have William Shakespeare's *Hamlet* and William Faulkner's *The Hamlet*, though, of course, with these examples the author's actual rights in regard to "his" text, as well as responsibilities for them, differ enormously from one another, and in neither is the text fully and unequivocally "his." But increasingly we have ceded authors unique rights to their texts, rights that the physical form of the book both articulates, celebrates, and exploits. These rights, of course, are not self-evident, but have developed through a process of ideological accretion that the printed book was not solely responsible for but which it did accelerate and make virtually irresistible.[39]

Clearly those rights did not yet quite exist in the historical moment in which Shakespeare's plays reached print. Nonetheless, for reasons that had more to do with commercial desire than with a commitment to intellectual property, Shakespeare's plays increasingly began to appear in forms that gave physical shape to the idea that control over their linguistic structure belonged to the author alone. The books in which the plays appeared affirmed them as "by William Shakespeare," or "corrected and augmented by W. Shakespeare," or finally, as "The Workes of William Shakespeare, containing all his Comedies, Histories, and Tragedies." The plays were advertised as "his"; and whatever alteration they may have endured, this was putatively at his hand too.

At least once the plays had migrated from the necessarily collaborative economies of the theater itself and established themselves in the possessive realm of literature, Shakespeare's presumptive authority over them became absolute – hence the scorn for the "bad quartos" of the sixteenth century, or for the Restoration adaptations, or for the bowdlerization of the nineteenth century. Authors, of course, may modify, supplement, or cut their own texts, but should some other agent transfigure the authorial text it is an illegitimate act of interference, hence deserving the outrage. Once an author becomes an Author, staking a claim to a text or having it staked for him, the text becomes inviolable: our culture recognizes, as Raffaele Simone says, the "reader's right to interpret the text but not to touch it, that is to alter the body" ("The Body of the Text," p. 241).

The text, then, at least as a linguistic structure, belongs to its author, or so the book says, an author who affirms it as his or her own with an implicit assertion of its integrity, that is, both its originality and completeness. And the body of that text is, therefore, supposed to remain pure, uncontaminated by other bodies unless they have been formally invited in. There is a moral logic here, deeply compelling to me (though more, I suppose, as the father of a teenage daughter than as a Shakespearean or a historian of the book). From a textual point of view, however, it is a logic completely false, if not to all writing certainly to the nature of the drama, in which the author's text is necessarily open to the invited or uninvited attentions of all those people responsible for its performance. Of all literary forms the drama is the one least respectful of an author's literary ambitions. Nonetheless, the printed drama gives that ambition voice (and, in the case of Shakespeare, voices an ambition to which he himself never admitted).

It is that voice that we hear as the "real presence" that is thought to be betrayed in the electronic medium, but even in print, it should be clear, it is not very real. It is, as in Nathaniel Butter's 1608 *King Lear* quarto, or even in Jaggard's and Blount's 1623 folio, a presence, however insistently asserted, self-consciously constructed in type by the commercial ambition of the book trade. If authors do not actually write books, in the early seventeenth-century bookshop, as in today's, they do help to sell them.

The truth is that all of the technologies of writing betray "real presence"; always they offer a simulacrum of a voice that is by definition absent. The preference then of one over another cannot be based on some presumption of its greater authenticity. And even the pencil, it is worth reminding ourselves, is no more natural a writing tool than the computer. It is just a lot easier to understand how it works and its traces are more directly linked back to their author; that is, they are dependent less upon other agencies than are print or digital display, but not therefore any less mediations of the author's words.

The written word advertises authorial presence in the autograph hand that delivers the word to paper – as we have seen, for Shakespeare that is at most the 146 lines of *Sir Thomas More* and the seven surviving signatures. The book advertises it in its physical integrity and typographic claims of authorship – for Shakespeare achieved by suppressing the necessary collaborations of the playhouse and his own manifest indifference to print. The electronic text advertises it in the ability of the medium to represent the text not as a mere document but as an event – for Shakespeare by embedding the dramatic text in a network of additional textual and visual materials modeling the drama's own fundamental reality as a multi-media and variable ensemble of practices.

The ironies are obvious enough: there are no manuscripts, Shakespeare was, for the most part, uninterested in print, and of course he was a stranger to digitization. None of the forms in which we can read Shakespeare is authentic.[40] Nor can this be taken as a grudging admission that only in the theater is that authenticity found, for the theater from the first has always been willing to sacrifice presence to performance considerations, the author's text merely a script to be played and played with, an occasion to engage and display the talents of other theatrical artists all of whom impose their desires upon the text.

In the shift from codex to computer we will not lose Shakespeare, but neither we will find him in some more authentic way. As I have been arguing throughout this book, he has never really been in *any* of those textual spaces where we pretend he resides. Nonetheless, we endow each of them with his name, discovering in the various forms of their materiality imagined signs of his presence.[41] We are a bit like Hamlet, looking at a ghost that according to everything he has been taught cannot be his father's spirit. It stands before him in "questionable shape," yet nonetheless the Prince decides to recognize in the apparition an authenticity his Wittenberg education, anyhow, should tell him is impossible: "I'll call thee Hamlet, / King, father, royal Dane" (1.4.44–5). Looking at the various questionable shapes in which the plays appear to us, we too are motivated (and like Hamlet, more by desire than by knowledge) to find behind the "solid" or "sallied" texts, displayed in whatever media in which we encounter them, a ghostly presence that we call Shakespeare.

Notes

INTRODUCTION

1 William J. Mitchell, *City of Bits: Space, Place, and the Infobahn* (Cambridge, Mass.: MIT Press, 1995), p. 56.

2 D. F. McKenzie, "History of the Book," in *The Book Encompassed: Studies in Twentieth-Century Bibliography* (Cambridge: Cambridge University Press, 1992), p. 297. This is, of course, the principle articulated by Jerome J. McGann in *The Textual Condition* (Princeton: Princeton University Press, 1991). I have, obviously, been greatly influenced by McKenzie's and McGann's work, though McGann's account of the "text as a laced network of linguistic and bibliographic codes" (p. 13), however much it restores the text's physical aspects to the equation of meaning, seems to me too readily to occlude the actual agents responsible for the text's material being. For McGann often it sounds as if the "exchanges these two great semiotic systems work with each other" (p. 67) are themselves what create meaning rather than the productive activities of interested individuals. See also, E. A. Levenson, *The Stuff of Literature: Physical Aspects of Texts and Their Relation to Literary Meaning* (Albany: State University of New York Press, 1992).

3 René Wellek and Austin Warren, "The Mode of Existence of a Literary Work of Art," in *The Theory of Literature*, 3rd ed. (New York: Harcourt Brace, 1956), pp. 143–4.

4 The argument is made most powerfully by G. Thomas Tanselle. See his *Textual Criticism Since Greg: A Chronicle 150–1985* (Charlottesville: University of Virginia Press, 1987) and the elegant *A Rationale of Textual Criticism* (Philadelphia: University of Pennsylvania Press, 1989); but cf. below, chapter 4, pp. 117–20.

5 *The Prelude*, book 5, lines. 46–7.

6 Roger Chartier, *The Order of Books: Readers, Authors, and Libraries in Europe Between the Fourteenth and Eighteenth Centuries*, trans. Lydia G. Cochrane (Stanford: Stanford University Press, 1994), p. ix. See also D. F. McKenzie's *Bibliography and the Sociology of Texts* (London: British

Library, 1986), first conceived as the inaugural Panizzi Lectures at the British Library in 1985, a seminal work in bringing those "material effects" into view.

7 William Prynne, *Histrio-mastix* (London, 1633), sig. **6ᵛ.

8 M. C. Bradbrook, *The Rise of the Common Player: A Study of the Actor and Society in Shakespeare's England* (Cambridge, Mass.: Harvard University Press, 1964), p. 38.

9 Katherine Duncan-Jones has argued that the 1609 edition of the sonnets was printed from Shakespeare's own revised manuscript and was sold by Shakespeare to Thomas Thorpe; see her "Was the 1609 *Shake-speares Sonnets* Really Unauthorized?" *Review of English Studies* 34 (1983): 151–71. For reasons that are largely irrelevant here, I do not share the view that the volume represents another example of Shakespeare's commitment to print, though, even if it is, it does not affect my argument about Shakespeare's lack of interest in seeing his *plays* in print.

10 *William Shakespeare: The Complete Works*, ed. Stanley Wells and Gary Taylor (Oxford: Oxford University Press, 1986), p. xxxviii.

11 Michael Goldman, *Acting and Action in Shakespearean Tragedy* (Princeton: Princeton University Press, 1985), p. 15. See also, among the other very fine examples of performance-oriented criticism, Anthony Dawson, *Watching Shakespeare* (London: Macmillan, 1988); Robert Hapgood, *Shakespeare the Theatre-Poet* (Oxford: Oxford University Press, 1988); and Barbara Hodgdon, *The Shakespeare Trade: Performances and Appropriations* (Philadelphia: University of Pennsylvania Press, 1998). For an important study of the original conditions under which Shakespeare's plays were staged, see Alan C. Dessen, *Recovering Shakespeare's Theatrical Vocabulary* (Cambridge: Cambridge University Press, 1995).

12 See my "The Play(text)'s the Thing: Teaching Shakespeare (Not in Performance)," URL: <http://www.ardenshakespeare.com:9966/main/ardennet/>.

13 For two brilliant explorations of the complex relationship of print and performance, see W. B. Worthen's *Shakespeare and the Authority of Performance* (Cambridge: Cambridge University Press, 1997), esp. pp. 1–45; and Robert Weimann's *Author's Pen and Actor's Voice: Playing and Writing in Shakespeare's Theatre* (Cambridge: Cambridge University Press, 2000).

14 See Weimann's "Bifold Authority in Shakespeare's Theater," *Shakespeare Quarterly* 39 (1988): 401–17.

15 Stephen Orgel, "What is an Editor?" *Shakespeare Studies* 24 (1996): 23.

16 *Samuel Johnson on Shakespeare*, ed. H. R. Woudhuysen (Harmondsworth: Penguin, 1989), p. 136.

17 Terry Eagleton, *Criticism and Ideology* (London: Verso, 1978), p. 65.

18 John Aubrey, *"Brief Lives," chiefly of Contemporaries, set down by John Aubrey, between the Years 1669 & 1696*, ed. Andrew Clark (Oxford: Oxford University Press, 1898), vol. 2, p. 244.

19 See Malcolm Rogers, "The Meaning of Van Dyck's Portrait of Sir John Suckling," *Burlington Magazine* 120 (1978): 741–5.

I FROM PLAYHOUSE TO PRINTING HOUSE; OR, MAKING A GOOD IMPRESSION

1 As a number of textual scholars have observed, even this fixity has its limits, not least because of the proof-reading and correction process in the printing house, which would almost always result in every individual copy of a particular print run differing from all others in its arrangement of corrected and uncorrected sheets. Nonetheless, there is little evidence that contemporaries felt this fact, if they recognized it at all, as an unsettling of the printed text. Even when a publisher did call attention to the variant copies that existed, it is with remarkable equanimity, as in William Gouge's *The Whole-Armor of God* (1616), where the publisher's note on Errata says: "If therefore thou meete with any slippe that may make the sence obscure, compare the Boke with some others, and thou maist find it amended" (sig. A10ᵛ). Here the fact that copies differed does not disrupt the text's meaning but rather provides a way to secure it.

2 William Prynne, *Histrio-Mastix: the Players Scourge* (London, 1633), sig. **6ᵛ.

3 See Kari Konkola, "'People of the Book': The Production of Literary Texts in Early Modern England," *Publication of the Bibliographic Society of America* 94 (2000): 5–31, esp. p. 18, n. 26.

4 Peter W. M. Blayney, "The Publication of Playbooks," in *A New History of Early English Drama*, ed. John D. Cox and David Scott Kastan (New York: Columbia University Press, 1997), p. 389. See also Mark Bland, "The London Book-Trade in 1600," in *A Companion to Shakespeare*, ed. David Scott Kastan (Oxford: Blackwell, 1999), pp. 450–63.

5 *Letters of Thomas Bodley to Thomas James, First Keeper of the Bodleian Library*, ed. G. W. Wheeler (Oxford: Oxford University Press, 1926), pp. 219, 222. Two playbooks, however, did in fact find their way into the early collection of the Bodleian; the 1620 Library catalogue lists Robert Daborne's *A Christian Turn'd Turke* (1612) and Thomas Heywood's *The Four Prentices of London* (1615). Bodley had, of course, died in late January 1613, but as there are only these two plays in the collection by 1620 their presence seems more likely to be accidental than to mark a change of Library policy.

6 *The Three Parnassus Plays*, ed. J. B. Leishman (London: Nicholson and Watson, 1949), pp. 247–8. John Stephens, in his *Cynthia's Revenge* (London, 1613), speaks of authors who "gape after the drunken harvest of forty shillings, and shame the worthy benefactors of *Hellicon*" (sig. A2ᵛ); and George Wither, in *The Schollers Purgatory* (London, 1624), similarly notes that stationers "cann hyre for a matter of 40 shillings, some needy IGNORAMUS" (sig. I1ᵛ).

7 This analysis is obviously heavily indebted to Peter Blayney's extraordinary reconstruction of the economics of playbook publishing in his "The Publication of Playbooks," esp. pp. 405–13.

8 These figures were provided by Alan Farmer, who is presently completing a remarkable dissertation at Columbia University on play publication and circulation in the period.

9 George Wither, *The Schollers Purgatory* (London, 1624), sigs. B6ᵛ–7ʳ, H5ʳ.

10 Thomas Heywood, *An Apology for Actors* (London, 1612), sig. G4ʳ.

11 Alexander Roberts, *An Exposition Upon the Hundred and Thirtie Psalme* (London, 1610), sig. O4ʳ.

12 Blayney observes that "we have been too busy chasing imaginary pirates" to understand how play texts normally found their way into print ("The Publication of Playbooks," p. 394). Piracy, as Laurie E. Maguire notes, "relates technically to the circumstances of publication, where it means the infringement of one stationer's rights by another." See her *Shakespearean Suspect Texts: The "Bad" Quartos and their Contexts* (Cambridge: Cambridge University Press, 1996), p. 16. See also Cyril Bathurst Judge, *Elizabethan Book-Pirates* (Cambridge, Mass.: Harvard University Press, 1934).

13 Samuel Daniel, *The Vision of The Twelve Goddesses* (London, 1604), sig. A3ʳ.

14 Stephen Egerton, *A Lecture preached by Maister Egerton, at the Blacke-friers, 1589* (London, 1603), sig. A4ʳ.

15 Fredson Bowers, *On Editing Shakespeare and the Elizabethan Dramatists* (Philadelphia: University of Pennsylvania Press, 1955), p. 41.

16 For a full and richly suggestive account of the complex "textual situation" of *Hamlet*, see Leah Marcus, *Unediting the Renaissance: Shakespeare, Marlowe, Milton* (London: Routledge, 1996), pp. 132–76.

17 See Gerald D. Johnson, "Nicholas Ling, Publisher 1580–1607," *Studies in Bibliography* 37 (1985): 203–14. On such reservation of printing rights, see, for example, Arber III. 92, where Thomas Creede enters *The Cognizance of a True Christian* with a notation: "This copie to be alwaies printed for **Nicholas Linge** by the seid **Thomas Creede** as often as it shalbe printed."

18 STC 16743.2 and 16743.3, *A true bill of the whole number that hath died in the Cittie of London* (London, 1603). See Gerald D. Johnson, "John

Trundle and the Book-Trade 1603–1626," *Studies in Bibliography* 39 (1986), esp. pp. 191–2.

19 Vickers, "*Hamlet* by Dogberry: A Perverse Reading of the Bad Quarto," *Times Literary Supplement*, 24 December 1993, p. 5.

20 On this aspect of *Knight of the Burning Pestle*, see Zachary Lesser, "Walter Burre's *Knight of the Burning Pestle*," *English Literary Renaissance* 29 (1999): 22–43; *Troilus*, of course, was published in 1609, with two separate title pages, one announcing the play "*As it was acted by the Kings Maiesties* servants at the Globe," and one, with only the indication that was "*Written by* William Shakespeare" and printed with the publisher's advertisement claiming that it was a "new play" that was "neuer clapper-clawd with the palms of the vulger."

21 Some of this material on the *King Lear* title page appears in different form in my *Shakespeare after Theory* (New York: Routledge, 1999), pp. 37 and 81.

22 Few scholars believe *The Troublesome Reign* to be by Shakespeare, though W. J. Courthope insisted that "Shakespeare alone was the author." See his *History of English Poetry* (New York: Macmillan, 1903), vol. 4, p. 55. More recently, Eric Sams has similarly argued that the anonymous play is the apprentice work of the young Shakespeare. See his *The Real Shakespeare: Retrieving the Early Years, 1564–1594* (New Haven: Yale University Press, 1995), pp. 146–53. Although there are a number of verbal parallels, only two or three lines are identical in the two plays, which seems to rule out either play as an early version of the other. Scholars do believe, however, that one play is clearly indebted to the other, usually arguing that the anonymous, Queen's men play was the source of Shakespeare's history.

23 George Walton Williams has dated this edition 1622; see his "The Printer and the Date of *Romeo and Juliet* Q4," *Studies in Bibliography* 18 (1965): 253–4.

24 E. K. Chambers, *The Elizabethan Stage* (Oxford: Oxford University Press, 1923), vol. 3, p. 187; and *A Dictionary of Printers and Booksellers . . . 1557–1640*, gen. ed. R. B. McKerrow (London: Bibliographical Society, 1910), p. 84.

25 W. W. Greg, *Two Elizabethan Stage Abridgements: "The Battle of Alcazar" and "Orlando Furioso": An Essay in Critical Bibliography* (Oxford: Oxford University Press, 1923), p. 130.

26 D. Allen Carroll, "Who Wrote *Greenes Groats-worth of Witte* (1592)?" *Renaissance Papers 1992*, ed. George Walton Williams and Barbara J. Baines (Durham, NC: Southeast Renaissance Conference, 1993), p. 75.

27 *Records of the Court of the Stationers' Company, 1576–1602*, ed. W. W. Greg and E. Boswell (London: The Bibliographical Society, 1930), p. 21 (3

Nov. 1586); and *A Transcript of the Stationers' Registers*, ed. Edward Arber (London, 1875), vol. 2, p. 706 (30 Sept. 1589) (hereafter *SR*).

28 Greg and Boswell (eds.), *Records of the Court of the Stationers' Company*, pp. 46 and 56 (5 March 1593; 10 April 1597).

29 Henry R. Plomer, "The Printers of Shakespeare's Plays and Poems," *The Library*, 2nd series, 7 (1906): 153.

30 See W. Craig Ferguson, *Valentine Simmes* (Charlottesville: University of Virginia Press, 1968), pp. 86–9.

31 Harry Hoppe calculated 0.9 printer's mistakes per page in Q1 and 1.4 in Q2. See his *The Bad Quarto of "Romeo and Juliet": A Bibliographic and Textual Study* (Ithaca: Cornell University Press, 1948), pp. 8–9.

32 *The Complete Works of Shakespeare*, ed. David M. Bevington (New York: HarperCollins, 1992), p. A-14.

33 Greg and Boswell (eds.), *Records of the Court of the Stationers' Company*, p. 78 (7 July 1600).

34 Jill L. Levinson, editor of the new Oxford edition of *Romeo and Juliet*, asserts that Q1 "shows clear signs of connection with performance"; Q2, however, she argues, with its "duplication of several passages," shows the marks of "authorial revision" and therefore must be based on "authorial working papers rather than a manuscript used in the theatre." See her "Editing *Romeo and Juliet*: 'A challenge [,] on my life,'" in *New Ways of Looking at Old Texts, II*, ed. W. Speed Hill (Tempe: Medieval and Renaissance Text Society, 1998), esp. p. 69.

2   FROM QUARTO TO FOLIO; OR, SIZE MATTERS

1 "Upon *Aglaura* Printed in Folio," in *Parnassus Biceps, or, Several Choice Pieces of Poetry, 1656*, ed. G. Thorn-Drury (London: Etchells and Macdonald, 1927), pp. 57–8.

2 Thomas Heywood, *The Rape of Lucrece*, (London, 1608), sig. A2^r.

3 Heywood, *Apology for Actors* (London, 1612), sig. A4^r.

4 W. W. Greg, *The Shakespeare First Folio: Its Bibliographic and Textual History* (Oxford: Oxford University Press, 1955), p. 2.

5 Greg, *The Editorial Problem in Shakespeare: A Survey of the Foundation of the Text*, 2nd ed. (Oxford: Oxford University Press, 1951), p. 157.

6 Preface to the 1765 edition of Shakespeare's plays, in *Samuel Johnson on Shakespeare*, ed. H. R. Woudhuysen (London: Penguin, 1989), p. 147. Andrew Murphy has also drawn attention to Johnson's and Greg's differing imagination of Shakespeare's thoughts in his retirement. See his "'To Ferret Out Any Hidden Corruption': Shakespearean Editorial Metaphors," *TEXT* 10 (1997): 202–4.

7 Heywood, *The English Traveller* (London, 1633), sig. A3^r; on Heywood's print ambitions, see Ben Robinson, "Thomas Heywood and the

Cultural Politics of Seventeenth-century Play Collections," forthcoming in *Studies in English Literature*.

8 E. K. Chambers, *William Shakespeare: Facts and Problems* (Oxford: Oxford University Press, 1930), vol. 2, p. 234. Sir Isaac Gollancz first called attention the poem; see his "Contemporary Lines to Heminge and Condell," in *Times Literary Supplement*, 26 January 1922, p. 56.

9 For an example of such a procedure, see J. W., "Original Letters of Jo. Davies," *Gentleman's Magazine* 60 (1790): 23–4, where the first four letters, from John Davies to Richard and Owen Wynne in 1628–29, concern Davies's proposal for a Welsh Dictionary that he wants to be circulated among the London stationers (along with his assurance that his hand is "faire" and "without many interlynings").

10 *Records of the Court of the Stationers' Company, 1602–1640*, ed. W. A. Jackson (London: The Bibliographical Society, 1957), p. 110.

11 See A. W. Pollard, *Shakespeare Folio and Quartos* (1909; rpt. New York: Cooper Square, 1970), pp. 81–104; Greg, *The Shakespeare First Folio*, pp. 9–17; Leo Kirschbaum, *Shakespeare and the Stationers* (Columbus: Ohio State University Press, 1955), pp. 227–42. The ten plays must have often been purchased as a group, as suggested by the similarity of their survival rates.

12 Algernon Charles Swinburne, *Studies in Prose and Poetry* (London: Chatto & Windus, 1894), p. 90.

13 For a printer, the size of the job would be of little concern, assuming his rates were set appropriately; indeed a large job would be an advantage, assuring consistent work. The publisher, however, assumed the financial risk of the project, fronting the costs for producing and wholesaling the books; for the publisher, then, the larger the project the greater the risk.

14 Quoted in Greg, *The Shakespeare First Folio*, pp. 3–4.

15 On the various activities of the book trade, see Laurie Maguire, "The Craft of Printing (1600)," in *A Companion to Shakespeare*, ed. David Scott Kastan (Oxford: Blackwell, 1999), pp. 434–49, esp. pp. 435–6.

16 R. Crompton Rhodes has a short account of Blount's career in his *Shakespeare's First Folio* (Oxford: Basil Blackwell, 1923), esp. pp. 47–51. In many ways the best study remains Sidney Lee's "An Elizabethan Bookseller," *Bibliographica* 1 (1895): 474–98. For a more comprehensive account of Blount's life and career, see Gary Taylor's forthcoming "Edward Blount, Publisher of Shakespeare."

17 Greg, *The Shakespeare First Folio*, p. 4.

18 Rhodes, in *Shakespeare's First Folio*, argues that Blount was the "head of the syndicate" (p. 48), and even Peter Blayney assumes that Blount and Issac Jaggard were the volume's "principal publishers" (Peter W. M. Blayney, *The First Folio of Shakespeare*, [Washington, D. C.: The Folger

Shakespeare Library, 1991] p. 2). Certainly by the time the volume appeared, they indeed were, but, as I am arguing here, I think it is most likely that Blount entered the consortium well after the project was conceived.

19 R. B. McKerrow, *A Dictionary of Printers and Booksellers in England, Scotland, and Ireland, 1557–1640* (London: The Bibliographical Society, 1910), p. 217. On Ponsonby, see Michael Brennan, "William Ponsonby: Elizabethan Stationer," *Analytic and Enumerative Bibliography* 7 (1983): 91–110.

20 See D. F. McKenzie, *Stationers' Company Apprentices, 1605–1640* (Charlottesville: Bibliographic Society of the University of Virginia, 1961), p. 45. Philip Townesend in July 1623 became the last apprentice who would be bound to Blount.

21 On 3 November 1624, Blount transferred his title to *Hero and Leander*, which had already been through eight editions at the time of the sale, to Samuel Vickers (*SR*, vol. 4, p. 126).

22 William A. Jackson (ed.), *Records of the Court of the Stationers' Company, 1602–1640* (London: The Bibliographical Society, 1957), p. 180.

23 Blount assigned his rights in eighteen plays by Shakespeare to Robert Allott on 16 November 1630 (*SR*, vol. 4. p. 243). On the sale of the bookshop, see Peter W. M. Blayney, *The Bookshops in Paul's Cross Churchyard* (London: The Bibliographical Society, 1990), pp. 26–7.

24 The second edition of the Jonson folio had to wait until 1640, three years after the playwright's death. In 1631, three plays that had not appeared in the original folio (*Bartholomew Fair, Staple of News, Devil is an Ass*) were published in folio formats as a supplement to the 1616 edition. In 1640, a new edition of the 1616 folio was published, and the collection of three plays was reissued that year by Richard Meighen, with a title page identifying it as "The second Volume." The publishing arrangements surrounding these events are enormously complicated and in some details still obscure. See W. P. Williams, "Chetwin, Crooke, and the Jonson Folios," *Studies in Bibliography* 30 (1977): 75–95.

25 Quoted in *Ben Jonson*, ed. C. H. Herford and Evelyn Simpson (Oxford: Oxford University Press, 1950), vol. 9, p. 13; Henry Fitzgeffrey, "Satyra prima," in *Satyres and Satyricall Epigrams* (London, 1617), sig. A8ʳ.

26 "Conversations with William Drummond," in Ben Jonson, *The Complete Poems*, ed. George Parfit (Harmondsworth: Penguin, 1975), p. 471.

27 Blayney, *The First Folio of Shakespeare*, pp. 21–4.

28 See Scott McMillin, *The Elizabethan Theatre and "The Book of Sir Thomas More"* (Ithaca: Cornell University Press, 1987); Trevor Howard-Hill (ed.), *Shakespeare and "Sir Thomas More": Essays on the Play and its*

Shakespearean Interest (Cambridge: Cambridge University Press, 1989); and *Shakespeare's Hand in "The Play of Sir Thomas More": Papers by Alfred W. Pollard, W. W. Greg, E. Maunde Thompson, J. Dover Wilson, and R. W. Chambers* (Cambridge: Cambridge University Press, 1923).

29 Stanley Wells and Gary Taylor, with John Jowett and William Montgomery, *William Shakespeare: A Textual Companion* (Oxford: Oxford University Press, 1987), p. 557. The edition itself was published in 1986.

30 James Spedding, "Who wrote Shakespeare's *Henry VIII*?" *Gentleman's Magazine*, n.s. 34 (1850): 115–24 381–2. Almost simultaneously, Samuel Hickson published a short piece with the same conclusion and also entitled "Who wrote Shakespeare's *Henry VIII?*" in *Notes and Queries* 43 (24 August 1850): 198.

31 Among the many attempts to establish the play's divided authorship, see Ants Oras, "Extra Monosyllables in *Henry VIII* and the Problem of Authorship," *Journal of English and German Philology* 52 (1935): 198–213; A. C. Partridge, *The Problem of "Henry VIII" Reopened* (Cambridge: Cambridge University Press, 1949); Robert Adger Law, "The Double Authorship of *Henry VIII*," *Studies in Philology* 56 (1959): 471–88; Marco Mincoff, "*Henry VIII* and Fletcher," *Shakespeare Quarterly* 12 (1961): 239–60; MacDonald P. Jackson, "Affirmative Particles in *Henry VIII*," *Notes and Queries* 207 (1962): 372–4; and, most recently and authoritatively, Jonathan Hope, *The Authorship of Shakespeare's Plays: A Socio-linguistic Study* (Cambridge: Cambridge University Press, 1994), esp. pp. 70–83.

32 *Macbeth*, however, will appear in the *Collected Works of Thomas Middleton*, an edition that Gary Taylor has supervised for Oxford University Press.

33 For the fullest account of the revision of the plays, see Grace Iopollo, *Revising Shakespeare* (Cambridge, Mass.: Harvard University Press, 1991).

34 A bit of evidence for single authorship – or at least for the continuity within the theatrical community of belief in that authorship – may be found in 1708 in John Downes's *Roscius Anglicanus*, ed. Montague Summers (1929; rpt. New York: Benjamin Blom, 1968). Downes praises Betterton's performance of Henry VIII as "so right and justly done," Betterton having been "Instructed in it by Sir *William* [Davenant], who had it from old Mr. *Lowen*, that had his Instructions from Mr. *Shakespear* himself" (p. 24).

35 See Margreta de Grazia, *Shakespeare Verbatim* (Oxford: Clarendon Press, 1991), pp. 14–48; and Leah Marcus, *Puzzling Shakespeare: Local Reading and its Discontents* (Berkeley: University of California Press, 1988), pp. 2–25, 43–50. See also Stephen Orgel's seminal essay, "The Authentic Shakespeare," *Representations* 21 (1988): 1–25.

36 "Ode to Himself," *Ben Jonson*, ed. Herford and Simpson, vol. 6, p. 492.

37 The Stationers, "out of their zeale to the advancement of learning," agreed, at the request of Bodley, to deposit one copy of every book published by a company member, on the condition that any could be borrowed if required for reprinting. In the event, many stationers, in spite of various efforts to strengthen the arrangement with fines for non-compliance, simply declined to make books available. See Ian Philips, *The Bodleian Library in the Seventeenth and Eighteenth Centuries* (Oxford: Oxford University Press, 1983), pp. 27–9; see also Robert C. Barrington Partridge, *History of the Legal Deposit of Books Throughout the British Empire* (London: The Library Association, 1938), p. 289.

38 See the photograph of Dering's account book in Blayney, *The First Folio of Shakespeare*, p. 25.

39 An earlier version of the argument of the remainder of this chapter appears in my *Shakespeare After Theory* (New York: Routledge, 1999), pp. 87–91.

40 A. W. Pollard, *Shakespeare's Fight with the Pirates* (Cambridge: Cambridge University Press, 1920), pp. 45–6.

41 See Margreta de Grazia, "The Essential Shakespeare and the Material Text," *Textual Practice* 1 (1988), esp. pp. 72–7; and Paul Werstine, "Narratives about Printed Shakespeare Texts: 'Foul Papers' and 'Bad' Quartos," *Shakespeare Quarterly* 41 (1990): 65–86.

42 While Chambers, for example, calls Busby "chief of the surreptitious printers" (*The Elizabethan Stage* [Oxford: Oxford University Press, 1923], vol. 3, p. 191), his practice here seems neither unusual nor improper. See Gerald D. Johnson's "John Busby and the Stationers' Trade," *The Library*, 6th series, 7 (1985): 1–15, one of a series of excellent essays Johnson has written on early modern publishers. Johnson argues that there is nothing irregular about the double entrance of the play: Busby buys and enters the play with the aim only of selling the rights, which he subsequently does to Arthur Johnson. Only the fact that this sale happens immediately after Busby's own registration of the play (or that both sales took place earlier and were belatedly registered together) produces the unusual double entry and the illusion of some underhanded dealing.

43 Edmond Malone (ed.), *The Plays and Poems of William Shakspeare* (London, 1790), vol. 1, p. xii.

44 Though Pollard, for example, puts great weight on the accuracy of this description (*Shakespeare's fight with the Pirates*, pp. 59–61), it is worth recalling that Humphrey Moseley in his epistle to the Readers in the 1647 Beaumont and Fletcher folio claims similarly that "Mr. Fletchers owne hand, is free from interlining; and his friends affirme he never writ any one thing twice: it seemes he had that rare felicity

to prepare and perfect all first in his owne braine; to shape and attire his Notions, to adde or loppe off, before he committed one word to writing, and never touched pen till all was to stand as firme and immutable as if ingraven in Brasse or Marble." Even a glance at a page of Fletcher's autograph will reveal the conventional flattery of Moseley's lines.

45 It is, of course, Blount who had the greatest financial vulnerability in the project – Smethwick and Aspley probably having contributed their titles as the greatest part of their investment, and Jaggard still with a thriving printing business.

46 Jeffrey Masten writes similarly that "'seventeenth-century authors' did not exist independently of their construction in the textual materials we read" See his remarkable *Textual Intercourse: Collaboration, Authorship, and Sexualities in Renaissance Drama* (Cambridge: Cambridge University Press, 1997), esp. pp. 113–55 (quotation on p. 120).

47 Richard Dutton also sees Shakespeare as "a company man" in his fine essay, "The Birth of an Author," in *Texts and Cultural Change in Early Modern England*, ed. Cedric C. Brown and Arthur F. Marotti (New York: St. Martin's Press, 1997), pp. 153–78.

3 FROM CONTEMPORARY TO CLASSIC; OR, TEXTUAL HEALING

1 The best account of the issue of title to Shakespeare's plays still remains Giles E. Dawson's "The Copyright of Shakespeare's Dramatic Works," in *Studies in Honor of A. H. R. Fairchild*, ed. Charles T. Prouty (Columbia: University of Missouri Press, 1946), pp. 11–35.

2 *SR*, vol. 4, p. 182.

3 Pavier assignment: 4 Aug. 1626: *SR*, vol. 4, p. 165; Bird assignment: 8 Nov. 1630: *SR* vol. 4, p. 242.

4 Blount assignment: 16 Nov. 1630: *SR*, vol. 4, p. 243.

5 Walkely to Hawkins: 1 March 1627/8: *SR*, vol. 4, p.194; Johnson to Meighen: 29 Jan. 1629/30: *SR* vol. 4, p. 227.

6 Edmond Malone (ed.), *The Plays and Poems of William Shakespeare* (London, 1790), vol. 1, p. xliii; Samuel Johnson and George Steevens (eds.), *The Plays of William Shakespeare* (London, 1793), vol. 1, p. xxviii.

7 Matthew Black and Matthias Shaaber, *Shakespeare's Seventeenth-century Editors, 1632–1685* (New York: MLA, 1937), p. 32.

8 *The Works of William Shakespeare*, ed. W. G. Clarke and John Glover (Cambridge and London: Macmillan, 1863), vol. 1, p. xi.

9 A. W. Pollard, *Shakespeare Folios and Quartos: A Study of the Bibliography of Shakespeare's Plays* (London: Methuen, 1909), p. 158.

10 For an account of the efforts to close the theaters, see my "'Publike

Sports' and 'Publike Calamities': Plays, Playing, and Politics," in *Shakespeare After Theory* (New York: Routledge, 1999), pp. 201–20.

11 Ric. Brome [*sic*], dedicatory poem to Beaumont and Fletcher, *Comedies and Tragedies* (London, 1647), sig. E1ʳ.

12 And indeed they dominated the stage as well, two of their plays, as Dryden said in his *Essay of Dramatick Poesie* (1668), "being acted throughout the year for one of *Shakespeare*'s or *Jonson*'s." Quoted in *Shakespeare: The Critical Heritage*, ed. Brian Vickers (London and Boston: Routledge, Kegan and Paul, 1974), vol. 2, p. 139. Anyone working on Shakespeare's reputation is indebted to the work of Vickers in compiling the six volumes of this project.

13 Heylyn, *Cosmographie* (London, 1652), sig. Zz2ᵛ.

14 *The Diary of the Rev. John Ward*, ed. Charles Severn (London: H. Colburn, 1839), p. 41.

15 "The Booksellers to the Reader" (signed John Martyn, Henry Herringham, and Richard Mariot), *The Wild-Goose Chase* (London, 1652). The note is repeated in the second Beaumont and Fletcher folio, *Fifty Comedies and Tragedies* (London, 1679), sig. A1ᵛ.

16 Quoted in Vickers (ed.) *Shakespeare: The Critical Heritage*, vol. 2, p. 94.

17 See, for example, Jean I. Marsden's thoughtful study, *The Re-Imagined Text: Shakespeare, Adaptation, and Eighteenth-Century Literary Theory* (Lexington: University Press of Kentucky, 1995); as well as Hazelton Spencer, *Shakespeare Improved* (Cambridge, Mass.: Harvard University Press, 1925); and Gunner Sorelius, *"The Giant Race Before the Flood": Pre-Restoration Drama on the Stage and in the Criticism of the Restoration* (Upsala: Almqvist & Wiksells, 1966).

18 *Diary of John Evelyn*, ed. E. S. De Beer (Oxford: Oxford University Press, 1955), vol. 3, p. 304.

19 "Prologue" (line 24) to *The Tempest, or The Enchanted Island: A Comedy* in *The Works of John Dryden*, vol. 10, ed. Maxmillian E. Novak (Berkeley: University of California Press, 1970), p. 6; "Preface to the Play," *Troilus and Cressida, or, Truth Found Too Late*, in *The Works of John Dryden*, vol. 13, ed. Maxmillian E. Novak (Berkeley: University of California Press, 1984), p. 226.

20 On the politics of the play, see Nancy Maguire, "Nahum Tate's *King Lear*: 'The King's Blest Restoration,'" in *The Appropriation of Shakespeare: Post-Renaissance Reconstruction of the Works and the Myth*, ed. Jean I. Marsden (Hemel Hempstead: Harvester Wheatsheaf, 1991), pp. 29–42.

21 John Downes, *Roscius Anglicanus*, ed. Montague Summers (1929; New York: Benjamin Blom, 1968), p. (22).

22 *Samuel Johnson on Shakespeare*, ed. Henry Woudhuysen (Harmondsworth: Penguin, 1989), p. 222. Steevens is quoted in Vickers (ed.), *Shakespeare:*

The Critical Heritage, vol. 6, p. 59, from an unsigned essay, "Observations on the plays altered from Shakespeare," in *St. James Chronicle* (13–16 March 1779).

23 George Colman, *The History of King Lear* (London, 1768), p. iv.

24 Brian Vickers, *Returning to Shakespeare* (London: Routledge, 1989), p. 229.

25 H. N. Hudson, *Lectures on Shakespeare, II* (New York: Baker and Scribner, 1848), pp. 277–8.

26 *The Works of Mr. Francis Beaumont, and Mr. John Fletcher* (London, 1711), vol. 1, p. viii.

27 Preface to *Troilus and Cressida*, in *Works of John Dryden*, vol. 13, p. 225.

28 Quoted in Colin Franklin, *Shakespeare Domesticated: The Eighteenth-century Editions* (Aldershot: Scolar, 1991), p. 194.

29 The phrase here is Warburton's, from his Preface to *The Works of Shakespear* (London, 1747), vol. 1, p. xvi.

30 Downes, *Roscius Anglicanus*, p. (17).

31 The document is reproduced in Allardyce Nicoll, *A History of English Drama*, 4th ed. (Cambridge: Cambridge University Press, 1961), vol. 1. pp. 352–3. See also John Freehafer, "The Formation of the London Patent Companies," *Theatre Notebook* 20 (1965): 6–30.

32 See Robert D. Hume, *The Development of English Drama in the Late Seventeenth Century* (Oxford: Oxford University Press, 1976), p. 20.

33 Downes, *Roscius Anglicanus*, p. (24).

34 William Rufus Chetwood, quoted in E. K. Chambers, *William Shakespeare: A Study of Facts and Problems* (Oxford: Oxford University Press, 1930), vol. 2, p. 254.

35 Marsden, *The Re-Imagined Text*, p. 1.

36 *The Tragedy of King Richard the II . . . Alter'd from Shakesper, by Mr. Theobald* (London, 1720), sig. A2^r.

37 Lewis Theobald, *Shakespeare Restored* (London, 1726), p. 165.

38 David Hume observes that "it is remarkable, that in all the historical plays of Shakespear . . . there is scarcely any mention of *civil Liberty*." See his *The History of England from the Invasion of Julius Caesar to the Revolution of 1688* (Indianapolis: Liberty Classics, 1983), vol. 4, p. 386n.

39 Many, of course, have thought *Double Falsehood* a forgery by Theobald, rather than a revision. See Walter Graham's edition of the play (Cleveland: Western Reserve University Press, 1920), esp. pp. 9–11; though see also Brean S. Hammond,'s "Theobald's *Double Falsehood*: An 'Agreeable Cheat'?" *Notes and Queries* 31 (1984): 2–3, for an argument that Theobald indeed had a seventeenth-century manuscript that he revised for the stage.

40 The advertisement is cited in Robert Hume's "Before the Bard: 'Shakespeare' in Early Eighteenth-century London," *ELH* 64 (1997): 46.

41 In the first half-century following the restoration of the monarchy, playbills and other advertisements did not generally attribute authorship. In the eighteenth century, however, Shakespeare's name increasingly was included on playbills, but his name there offered no guarantee that his work was being performed in unaltered form. See Hume's "Before the Bard: 'Shakespeare' in Early Eighteenth-century London," esp. pp. 44–5.

42 András Kiséry has brilliantly explored the historically determined implications of calling editions "Works" in an as yet unpublished essay, "'Authorities from Himself': Shakespeare's *Works*."

43 The case of Donaldson v. Beckett had focused attention on the monopoly of the booksellers, and the Lords' decision in that case turned copyright into an author's right instead of the publisher's right, as it had been. See Mark Rose, *Authors and Owners: The Invention of Copyright* (Cambridge, Mass: Harvard University Press, 1993). On the Tonsons, see below, pp. 98–101.

44 J. P. Genest, *Some Account of the English Stage from the Restoration in 1660 to 1830* (Bath: Thomas Rodd, 1832), vol. 6, p. 439.

45 On play publication that was tied to theatrical auspices in the late seventeenth and early eighteenth centuries, see Laurie E. Osborne, "Rethinking the Performance Editions: Theatrical and Textual Productions of Shakespeare," in *Shakespeare, Theory, and Performance*, ed. James C. Bulman (London and New York: Routledge, 1996), pp. 168–86.

46 John Dryden, "Preface," *All for Love, or, The World Well Lost*, in *The Works of John Dryden*, vol. 13, p. 18. On the religious language and sentiment surrounding the reception of Shakespeare, see Péter Dávidházi, *The Romantic Cult of Shakespeare: Literary Reception in Anthropological Perspective* (Houndsmill, Basingstoke: Macmillan, 1998).

47 "Sweet Shakespeare" from W[illiam] C[ovell], *Polimanteia* (1595), in *The Shakspere Allusion-Book*, rev. John Munro (1909; Freeport, New York: Books for Libraries Press, 1970), vol. 1, p. 23 (also, of course, Jonson's famous "Sweet Swan of Avon"); "mellifluous *Shake-speare*" from Thomas Heywood, *The Hierarchie of the Blessed Angels* (1635), in *The Shakspere Allusion-Book*, vol. 1, p. 393 (and also Meres's "mellifluous & hony-tongued *Shakespeare*"); "Ingenious Shakespeare," anon., from *Choyce Drollery, Songs, and Sonnets* (1652), in *The Shakspere Allusion-Book*, vol. 1, p. 280; "copious Shakepear," in Francis Kirkman's dedicatory epistle to *The Loves and Adventures of Clerio and Lozia* (1652), in *The Shakspere Allusion-Book*, vol. 2, p. 24 (and Webster also notes Shakespeare's "copious industry" in the preface to *The White Devil*); "Immortal Shakespeare," Nathanial Lee, *Mithradites*, preface, in *The Shakspere Allusion-Book*, vol. 2, p. 264; "Godlike Shakespear," Thomas

Betterton, epilogue to *The Prophetess*, in *The Shakspere Allusion-Book*, vol. 2, p. 338. Murphy, in *Grays-Inn Journal* (28 July 1753), quoted in Vickers, (ed.), *Shakespeare: The Critical Heritage: The Story of Shakespeare's Reputation*, vol. 4, p. 93; and "lay bible" is Henry Morley's phrase, quoted in Louis Marder, *His Exits and Entrances* (Philadelphia and New York: J. B. Lippincott, 1963), p. 18.

48 Marcus Walsh, *Shakespeare, Milton, and Eighteenth-century Literary Editing: The Beginnings of Interpretive Scholarship* (Cambridge: Cambridge University Press, 1997), esp. pp. 111–98; and Simon Jarvis, *Scholars and Gentlemen: Shakespearian Textual Criticism and Representations of Scholarly Labour, 1725–1765* (Oxford: Oxford University Press, 1995), esp. pp. 17–20.

49 Alexander Pope (ed.), "Preface" in *Works of Shakespear* (London, 1725), vol. 1, p. xxii; Lewis Theobald (ed.), "The Preface," in *The Works of Shakespeare in Seven Volumes* (London, 1733), vol. 1, p. xl.

50 Quoted in Marder, *His Exits and His Entrances*, p. 18.

51 Michael Dobson, *The Making of the National Poet: Shakespeare, Adaptation and Authorship* (Oxford: Oxford University Press, 1992). See also Gary Taylor's deliciously picaresque history of Shakespeare's reputation: *Reinventing Shakespeare: A Cultural History from the Restoration to the Present* (New York: Vintage, 1991), esp. pp. 7–161.

52 *The London Gazette*, 14–17 March 1709; quoted in Alfred Jackson, "Rowe's Edition of Shakespeare," *The Library*, fourth series, 10 (1929–30): 455.

53 Nicholas Rowe (ed.), *The Works of Mr. William Shakespeare* (London, 1709), vol. 1, sig. A3ᵛ.

54 See Giles Dawson, "The Copyright of Shakespeare's Dramatic Works," p. 25. Also see Terry Bellinger, "Tonson, Wellington and the Shakespeare Copyrights," in *Studies in the Book Trade in Honour of Graham Pollard*, ed. R. W. Hunt, I. G. Philip, and R. J. Roberts (Oxford: Oxford Bibliographic Society, 1975), pp. 195–209. On Jacob Tonson's publishing career in general, see Harry M. Geduld, *Prince of Publishers: A Study of the Work and Career of Jacob Tonson* (Bloomington: University of Indiana Press, 1969).

55 Oddly, given his position as the first in the lineage of Shakespeare's professional editors, Rowe's editorial work has been much less carefully studied than that of many of his successors. For two valuable exceptions, see Barbara A. Mowat, "Nicholas Rowe and Twentieth-Century Shakespeare Text," in *Shakespeare and Cultural Traditions: The Selected Proceedings of the International Shakespeare Association World Congress, Tokyo, 1991*, ed. Tetsuo Kishi, Roger Pringle, and Stanley Wells (Newark, Del.: Associated University Presses, 1994), pp. 314–22; and Peter Holland, "Modernizing Shakespeare: Nicholas Rowe and *The Tempest*," *Shakespeare Quarterly* 51 (2000): 24–32.

56 Quoted in F. E. Halliday, *The Cult of Shakespeare* (London: Duckworth, 1957), p. 45.
57 *Evening Post*, 21 October 1721; quoted in Arthur Sherbo, *The Birth of Shakespeare Studies: Commentators from Rowe (1709) to Boswell-Malone (1821)* (East Lansing, Mich.: Colleagues Press, 1986), p. 2.
58 Letter to Jacob Tonson, Jr. (May 1772), in *The Correspondence of Alexander Pope*, ed. George Sherburn (Oxford: Oxford University Press, 1956), vol. 2. p. 118.
59 *The Evening Post*, 5 May 1722; quoted in Sherbo, *The Birth of Shakespeare Studies*, p. 2.
60 *Samuel Johnson on Shakespeare*, ed. Woudhuysen, p. 149.
61 For a thoughtful consideration of Pope's editing, see John A. Hart, "Pope as Scholar-Editor," *Studies in Bibliography* 23 (1970): 45–59; and, perhaps most positively of those who have written on Pope as an editor, A. D. J. Brown, "The Little Fellow Has Done Wonders," *Cambridge Quarterly* 21 (1992): 120–49.
62 See Peter Seary's sympathetic account of Theobald's achievement, *Lewis Theobald and the Editing of Shakespeare* (Oxford: Oxford University Press, 1990), esp. pp. 65–86, 171–98; see also R. F. Jones, *Lewis Theobald: His Contribution to English Scholarship, with some Unpublished Letters* (New York: Columbia University Press, 1919). For a more temperate consideration of Theobald's editorial practice, see Jarvis, *Scholars and Gentlemen*, pp. 94–106.
63 On the cash payment, see Tonson's accounts "Paid for the Editors of Shakespear," Folger MS. S. a. 163, reproduced in David Foxon, *Pope and the Early-Eighteenth Century Book Trade* (Oxford: Oxford University Press, 1991), p. 90. For the copies that added considerably to Theobald's compensation, and for the effect of the expiring copyright upon the negotiations, see Geduld, *Prince of Publishers*, pp. 143–4.
64 See Richard Corballis, "Copy-Text for Theobald's Shakespeare," *The Library*, 6th series, 8 (1986): 156–9; Theobald, *Works*, 1733, vol. 7, sig. Hh8ʳ.
65 Seary, *Lewis Theobald*, pp. 133–5; see also Hay Campbell's statement that "*Shakespear*'s works have been published by a number of persons in England; by Mr. Rowe, Mr. Theobald, Sir Thomas Hanmer, Mr. Samuel Johnson, &c, and if we can believe what these critics say of one another, their alterations are oftener for the worse than the better; yet, bad as they are, they carry along with them a property in the book thus manufactured . . ." (Quoted in Margreta de Grazia, *Shakespeare Verbatim: The Reproduction of Authenticity and the 1790 Apparatus* [Oxford: Oxford University Press, 1991], p. 194). Campbell argues that, thus, "each critic becomes proprietor of a work he was never capable of writing himself," but it was the Tonson family that secured proprie-

torship over Shakespeare's works through the editorial activities of the editors. It cannot be accidental that Rowe's edition, first in the sequence of Tonson Shakespeares, was published in the very year the copyright statute was being enacted, and is the first edition, as de Grazia notes, "with a named editor" (p. 192). And when the family sold off its copyrights in 1767, they did so as if the plays were "Tonson property to keep or assign in perpetuity" (p. 193).

66 *Samuel Johnson on Shakespeare*, ed. Woudhuysen, p. 150.

67 Letter to Warburton, 8 April 1729; in *Illustrations of the Literary History of the Eighteenth Century*, ed. John Nicholls (London, 1817), vol. 2, pp. 209–10.

68 W. W. Greg, *The Editorial Problem in Shakespeare: A Survey of the Foundations of the Text*, 3rd ed. (Oxford: Oxford University Press, 1954), p. 3. See, for example, Theobald's justification for emending the folio's "first of March" in *Julius Caesar*, 2.1.40 to "Ides of March" (*Works*, 1733, vol. 6, p. 143), where he discusses the manuscript contraction that must be responsible for "the corruption of the Text."

69 Isobel Grundy, "New Verse by Henry Fielding," *PMLA* 87 (1972): 244.

70 Peter Alexander, "Restoring Shakespeare: The Modern Editor's Task," *Shakespeare Survey* 5 (1952): 2.

71 De Grazia, *Shakespeare Verbatim*, p. 4. For a general overview of the achievement of the eighteenth-century editors, see R. B. McKerrow, "Shakespeare's Text by his Earlier Editors (1709–1768)," in *"Studies in Shakespeare" British Academy Lectures*, ed. Peter Alexander (Oxford: Oxford University Press, 1964), pp. 103–31; Grace Ioppolo, "'Old' and 'New' Revisionists: Shakespeare's Eighteenth-Century Editors," *Huntington Library Quarterly* 52 (1989): 347–61; Colin Franklin's invaluable *Shakespeare Domesticated: The Eighteenth-century Editions* (Aldershot: Scolar, 1991); and Paul Werstine, "Shakespeare," in *Scholarly Editing: A Guide to Research*, ed. D. C. Greetham (New York: MLA, 1995), esp. pp. 256–64.

72 *Samuel Johnson on Shakespeare*, ed. Woudhuysen, pp. 154–5.

73 Quoted in Vickers (ed.), *Shakespeare: The Critical Heritage*, vol. 6, p. 49.

74 *English Review* 3 (1784): 179. For a sensitive account of the cultural logic of the layout of the variorum page, see Joanna Gonderis, "'All This Farrago': The Eighteenth-century Shakespeare Variorum Page as a Critical Structure," in *Reading Readings: Essays on Shakespeare Editing in the Eighteenth Century*, ed. Gonderis (Cranbury, NJ: Associated University Presses, 1998), pp. 123–39.

75 While this is not the place for an extended discussion of Garrick, the great actor's actual commitment to authentic Shakespeare has been often overstated. An anonymous poem in the *London Magazine* of 1750 (June, p. 279) has Shakespeare's ghost praising Garrick as "my great

restorer" and complimenting the actor for refusing to "yield [him] up to Cibber and to Tate." Garrick, however, was no less an "improver" of Shakespeare than those men, although he adopted for the theater a passionate language of authenticity. His heavily revised version of *The Winter's Tale*, for example, eliminating most of Shakespeare's first three acts, was ironically introduced with a prologue expressing Garrick's desire "to lose no drop of this immortal man" (line 55). See George Winchester Stone, "Garrick's Long Lost Adaptation of *Hamlet*," *PMLA* 49 (1834): 890–921.

76 Griffiths, quoted in Vickers (ed.), *Shakespeare: The Critical Heritage*, vol. 5, p. 1; Steevens (ed. with Samuel Johnson), *The Complete Plays of William Shakespeare* (London, 1793), vol. 1, p. xi.

77 *The Correspondence of Thomas Percy and Edmond Malone*, ed. Arthur Tillotson (Baton Rouge: Louisiana University Press, 1944), pp. 238–42.

78 Quoted by Marder from *The Saturday Review* (1863), in *His Exits and His Entrances*, p. 18.

79 Gary Taylor, in *Reinventing Shakespeare*, also observes that Keats's poem is transcribed into his copy of the facsimile; Taylor writes that the facsimile itself expresses "a characteristic Romantic desire to do away with fussy intermediaries, to overthrow the editors and commentators of the eighteenth century . . . to return to the imagined purity of a Renaissance font, typographical and metaphorical, that could bring them into direct spiritual contact with the poet himself" (p. 152).

80 *The Family Shakespeare* (London: J. Hatchard, 1807), vol. 1, p. vii.

4 FROM CODEX TO COMPUTER; OR, PRESENCE OF MIND

1 Among the many important recent studies of the effects of the early book trade upon the texts we read, see Douglas A. Brooks, *From Playhouse to Printing House: Drama and Authorship in Early Modern England* (Cambridge: Cambridge University Press, 2000); Jeffrey Masten, *Textual Intercourse: Collaboration, Authorship, and Sexualities in Renaissance Drama* (Cambridge: Cambridge University Press, 1997); Peter W. M. Blayney, "The Publication of Playbooks," in *New History of Early English Drama*, ed. John D. Cox and David Scott Kastan (New York: Columbia University Press, 1997), pp. 383–422; Leah Marcus, *Unediting the Renaissance: Shakespeare, Marlowe, Milton* (New York: Routledge, 1996); Margreta de Grazia and Peter Stallybrass, "The Materiality of the Shakespearean Text," *Shakespeare Quarterly* 44 (1993): 255–84; Stephen Orgel, "Acting Scripts, Performing Texts," in *Crisis in Editing*, ed. Randall McLeod (New York: AMS, 1993), pp. 251–94; and his seminal "What is a Text," *Research Opportunities in Renaissance*

Drama 26 (1981): 3–6; and what might be thought the point of origin of much of this work, E. A. J. Honigmann, *The Stability of Shakespeare's Texts* (London: Edward Arnold, 1965), which, if Honigmann had only had the foresight to add an "In" as a prefix to the second word of his title, might today be better recognized for its originality and influence.

2 Elizabeth L. Eisenstein, *The Printing Press as an Agent of Change* (Cambridge: Cambridge University Press, 1979). See also *The Advent of Printing: Historians of Science Respond to Elizabeth Eisenstein's "The Printing Press as an Agent of Change"*, ed. Peter F. McNally (Montreal: McGill University Graduate School of Library and Information Studies, 1987); and Adrian Johns, *The Nature of the Book: Print and Knowledge in the Making* (Chicago: University of Chicago Press, 1998).

3 Paul Duguid, "Material Matters: The Past and Futurology of the Book," in *The Future of the Book*, ed. Geoffrey Nunberg (Berkeley: University of California Press, 1996), p. 77; and J. David Bolter, *Writing Space: The Computer, Hypertext, and the History of Writing* (Hillsdale: Lawrence Erlbaum Associates, 1991), p. 21.

4 Stewart Brand, *The Media Lab: Inventing the Future at MIT* (New York: Viking, 1989), p. 202.

5 Steiner's romanticism is revealed in his expression of the danger of the electronic textual environment, his fear that the text will "lose its implosive powers within the echo chambers of the self." See his *Real Presences: Is There Anything in What We Say?* (Chicago: University of Chicago Press, 1989), p. 39; see also Sven Birkerts, *The Gutenberg Elegies: The Fate of Reading in an Electronic Age* (New York: Ballantine Books, 1994) for another passionate view of the dangers of the new technologies of print, which not only "are modifying the traditional roles of writer and reader" (p. 158), but also are responsible for "a dispersal of presence" (p. 227) that is eroding "some of the fundamental authority of the human itself" (p. 228). Richard Lanham similarly asserts that "our cultural vitals are isomorphic with the book," and calls for the creation of "an agency of the federal government to protect it," in his *The Electronic Word: Democracy, Technology, and the Arts* (Chicago: University of Chicago Press, 1993), p. 154.

6 No doubt others have used the phrase, but perhaps none earlier than Gerard Genette. See his "Structuralism and Literary Criticism," in *Figures of Literary Discourse*, trans. A. Sheridan (New York: Columbia University Press, 1982), p. 82.

7 Updike is quoted in John Pickering, "Hypermedia: When Will They feel Natural," in *Beyond the Book: Theory, Culture and the Politics of Cyberspace*, ed. Warren Cherniak, Marilyn Deegan and Andrew Gibson (Oxford: Office for Humanities Communication, 1996), p. 51.

8 Steve Silberman, "Ex Libris: The Joys of Curling Up With a Good

Digital Reading Device," *Wired* July 1998, p. 101. I thank Alan Farmer for passing this review on to me.

9 Bolter, *Writing Space: The Computer, Hypertext, and the History of Writing*, p. 31.

10 Michael Joyce, "A Feel for Prose: Interstitial Links and the Contours of Hypertext," *Writing on the Edge* 4.1 (1992): 87.

11 George P. Landow, *Hypertext: The Convergence of Contemporary Theory and Technology* (Baltimore: The Johns Hopkins University Press, 1992), p. 19.

12 Roger Stoddard, "Morphology and the Book from an American Perspective," *Printing History* 17 (1987): 2.

13 T. E. Hulme, *Speculations: Essays on Humanism and the Philosophy of Art*, ed. Herbert Read (London: Routledge and Kegan Paul, 1936), p. 224.

14 See, among the very fine studies in this area, what might be thought the subfield's foundational texts: D. F. McKenzie's *Bibliography and the Sociology of Texts* (London: British Library, 1986); Jerome J. McGann, *The Textual Condition* (Princeton: Princeton University Press, 1991); and Roger Chartier's *The Cultural Uses of Print in Early Modern France*, trans. Lydia G. Cochrane (Princeton: Princeton University Press, 1987).

15 See, for example, Randy McLeod's brilliant essay, "Spellbound," in *Play-Texts in Old Spelling: Papers from the Glandon Conference*, ed. G. B. Shand and Raymond C. Shady (New York: AMS Press, 1984), pp. 81–96.

16 For a rigorous account of many of the contested terms and concepts in textual theory, see Peter L. Shillingsburg, *Resisting Texts: Authority and Submission in Constructing Meaning* (Ann Arbor: University Of Michigan Press, 1997).

17 Michael Best, "From Book to Screen: A Window on Renaissance Electronic Texts," *Early Modern Literary Studies* 1.2 (August 1995): URL: <http://purl.oclc.org/emls/01–2/bestbook.html>.

18 G. Thomas Tanselle, "Textual Criticism and Deconstruction," *Studies in Bibliography* 43 (1990): 4; and Tanselle, *A Rationale of Textual Criticism* (Philadelphia: University of Pennsylvania Press, 1989), p. 69. To be fair, Tanselle maintains that the idea "that a work of literature employs an intangible medium" is "not platonic"; see his "Textual Criticism and Literary Sociology," *Studies in Bibliography* 44 (1991), p. 97, n. 18. But see also D. C. Greetham, *Theories of the Text* (Oxford: Oxford University Press, 1999), who insists on Tanselle's "platonic nostalgia" (p. 39).

19 McGann, *The Textual Condition*, p. 11.

20 R. B. McKerrow (ed.), *The Works of Thomas Nashe* (1904–10; Oxford: Blackwell, 1966), vol. 2, p. 197.

21 J. Dover Wilson, "The Task of Heminge and Condell," in *Studies in the First Folio* (London: Oxford University Press, 1924), p. 71.

22 W. W. Greg, *The Editorial Problem in Shakespeare: A Survey of the Foundations of the Text*, 3rd ed. (Oxford: Oxford University Press, 1954), p. x (italics in original).

23 Fredson Bowers, *On Editing Shakespeare* (Charlottesville: University of Virginia Press, 1966), p. 87. The four quotations in this paragraph represent a sampling of the major texts and tenets of the New Bibliography.

24 Stanley Wells, *Re-Editing Shakespeare for the Modern Reader* (Oxford: Oxford University Press, 1984), p. 50.

25 See Barbara A. Mowat, "The Problem of Shakespeare's Text(s)," *Shakespeare Jahrbuch* 132 (1996): 26–43, who compellingly argues that "finding 'the Author's Original Manuscripts' would give us only another possible text, another set of variants to consider, rather than 'the exact Reading'" (p. 33).

26 See Stephen Orgel's "What is an Editor?" *Shakespeare Studies* 24 (1996): 23–9; and my "The Mechanics of Culture: Editing Shakespeare Today", in *Shakespeare After Theory* (New York: Routledge, 1999), pp. 59–70.

27 The distinction is, of course, Tanselle's; see his *Rationale*, esp. pp. 37–8, 57–8, and 68–70. See also Paul Eggert's "Document and Text: The 'Life' of the Literary Work and the Capacities of Editing," *TEXT* 7 (1994): 1–24.

28 Landow, *Hypertext. The Convergence of Contemporary Critical Theory and Technology*, p. 61. See also Jerome McGann's "The Rationale of HyperText," available in a number of places, but perhaps most appropriately cited by its URL: <http://jefferson.village.Virginia.edu/public/jjm2f/rationale.html>.

29 See, for example, Roland Barthes, *S/Z* (1970), trans. Richard Miller (New York: Hill and Wang, 1975), pp. 5–6.

30 See Peter S. Donaldson, "Digital Archive as Expanded Text: Shakespeare and Electronic Textuality," in *Electronic Text: Investigations in Method and Theory*, ed. Kathryn Sutherland (Oxford: Oxford University Press, 1997), pp. 173–97; Peter Holland, "Authorship and Collaboration: The Problem of Editing Shakespeare," in *The Politics of the Electronic Text*, ed. Warren Cherniak, Caroline Davis, and Marilyn Deegan (Oxford: Office for Humanities Communication, 1993), pp. 17–23; and Philip Brockbank, "Towards a Mobile Text," in *The Theory and Practice of Text-Editing*, ed. Ian Small and Marcus Walsh (Cambridge: Cambridge University Press, 1992), pp. 90–106.

31 Patrick W. Connor, "Hypertext in the Last Days of the Book," *Bulletin of the John Rylands Library* 74 (1992): 20.

32 See above, chap. 2, p. 157.

33 Donaldson, "Digital Archive as Expanded Text: Shakespeare and Electronic Textuality," p. 174.

34 Perhaps unsurprisingly, Richard Knowles quotes "Wittgenstein's *mot*" in his essay on "Variorum Commentary," in *TEXT* 6 (1994): 41.

35 For a dark version of hypertext and digitization in general, see Gary Taylor's deliberately unmemorably titled, "c:\wp\file.txt 05:41 10–07–98," in *The Renaissance Text: Theory, Editing, Textuality*, ed. Andrew Murphy (Manchester: Manchester University Press, 2000), pp. 44–54. For a useful collection of essays more enthusiastically considering the effects of hypermedia technology, see *The Literary Text in the Digital Age*, ed. Richard J. Finneran (Ann Arbor: University of Michigan Press, 1996).

36 See Umberto Eco's "Afterward" to *The Future of the Book*, ed. Geoffrey Nunberg (Berkeley: University of California Press, 1996), p. 295.

37 John Lavagnino, "Electronic Editions and the Needs of Readers," in *New Ways of Looking at Old Texts, II*, ed. W. Speed Hill (Tempe, Ariz.: Renaissance English Text Society, 1998), p. 151.

38 Gregory Bateson, *Mind and Nature: A Necessary Unity* (New York: Bantam, 1980), p. 12.

39 On the cultural presuppositions surrounding the book, see Raffaele Simone's provocative essay, "The Body of the Text," in *The Future of the Book*, ed. Geoffrey Nunberg (Berkeley: University of California Press, 1996), esp. pp. 240–2. See also Mark Rose's invaluable study of the historical conditions establishing the modern conception of authorship: *Authors and Owners: The Invention of Copyright* (Cambridge, Mass.: Harvard University Press, 1993).

40 Again, see Steven Orgel's brilliant exploration of the differing claims to authenticity that both texts and performance make in his "The Authentic Shakespeare," *Representations* 21 (1988): 5–25.

41 See Andrew Murphy's suggestive essay, "'Came Errour Here by Mysse of Man': Editing and the Metaphysics of Presence," *Yearbook of English Studies* 29 (1999): 118–37.

Index

Page numbers in *italics* refer to illustrations.

Accidence (Stanbridge), 45
acting companies, 30
  collaboration in, 14–15, 16, 17, 20, 26,
    48, 68, 69, 71, 72, 74, 77, 78, 88, 119,
    134, 136
  playwrights and, 14–15, 16, 17, 20, 48,
    68, 69
  in Restoration England, 89–90
  scripts owned by, 17, 47, 68
  see also specific companies
Addison, Joseph, 88–89
Adorno, Theodor W., 111
Aeschylus, 88
Aglaura (Suckling), 51
Alexander, Peter, 102–3, 153*n*
Alexander, William, 62
Allde, Edward, 45
Alleyn, Edward, 14
Allot, Robert, 63, 79, 80, 144*n*
Antipodes, The (Brome), 20, 31–33
Antony and Cleopatra (Shakespeare), 65, 81
Apology for Actors, An (Heywood), 55
Arcadia (Greene), 48
Arcadia (Sidney), 62
Aspley, William, 60, 61, 78, 79, 80, 147*n*
Aubrey, John, 11, 139*n*
Auden, W. H., 119
authors, authorship, 22, 134–35
  acting companies and, 14–15, 16, 17, 20,
    48, 68, 69
  collaborative, 17, 64–72
  copyright lacked by, 23–24, 25, 52, 134,
    150*n*
  intentions of, 3–4, 5, 16, 17–20, 26, 73,
    86, 88, 91, 113, 116, 118–19, 120–23,
    127, 129, 135–36
  named on play title pages, 17, *18*, 19–20,

28, 30–31, *32*, 33–34, *34*, *37*, *39*, *43*,
    47–49, 55–57, *56*, 64, 71, 93, *94*, 134
  print publication sought by, 16–20,
    31–33, 71, 140*n*
  on quality of printed texts, 24, 25–26
  Shakespeare as emblem of, 14, 16,
    48–49, 63–64, 134
  single, 14–15, 16, 17, 68–71, 77, 78, 111,
    145*n*
  unauthorized publication and, 20,
    23–24, 25–26, 27, 29, 33–35, 52, 73, 74

"bad quartos," 26–30, 44, 45–47, 72–76,
    134
Baldwin, William, 10
ballads, 44, 63
Barnes, Barnabe, 19–20
Barnfield, Richard, 55
Barons' Wars (Drayton), 30
Barthes, Roland, 125, 157*n*
Bartholomew Fair (Jonson), 144*n*
Bateson, Gregory, 133, 158*n*
Bayley, Lewis, 10
Beaumont, Francis, 21, 67, 83, 84, 88, 148*n*
Beaumont and Fletcher folios, 67, 83,
    146*n*–47*n*, 148*n*
Bedford, Countess of, 25
Bell, John, 96
Bellinger, Terry, 151*n*
Bentley, Richard, 97
Best, Michael, 156*n*
Betterton, Thomas, 90, 145*n*, 150*n*–51*n*
Bevington, David M., 46, 142*n*
bibles, 5, 97
Bills of Mortality, 30
Bird, Robert, 66, 79–80, 147*n*
Birkerts, Sven, 155*n*

Black, Matthew, 80, 147*n*
Blackfriars playhouse, 8, 89
Blake, William, 121
Bland, Mark, 139*n*
Blayney, Peter W. M., 22, 23, 24–25, 64,
  139*n*, 140, 143*n*–44*n*, 146*n*, 154*n*
Blount, Edward, 40, 60, 65–66, 78, 79, 80,
  135, 143*n*–44*n*, 147*n*
  publishing career of, 61–63
Bodleian Library, 22, 72, 139*n*, 146*n*
Bodley, Thomas, 22, 139*n*, 146*n*
Bolter, J. David, 112, 127, 155*n*, 156*n*
Bondman, The (Massinger), 90
book, the, *see* print, printed books
book trade regulations, 23–24, 25–26, 45,
  57
Boswell, E., 141*n*–42*n*
Boswell, James, 103
Bowdler, Henrietta and Thomas, 109–10,
  134
Bowers, Fredson, 27, 118, 140*n*, 157*n*
Boyle, John, 79
Bradbrook, M. C., 6, 138*n*
Brand, Stewart, 112, 155*n*
Brennan, Michael, 144*n*
Brewster, Edward, 66, 79–80
Britaines Troy (Heywood), 24
Brockbank, Philip, 157*n*
Brome, Richard, 20, 31–33, 51, 83, 148*n*
Brooks, Douglas A., 154*n*
Brown, A. D. J., 152*n*
Bullock, Mrs., 92
Burbage, Richard, 14, 54–55
Burby, Cuthbert, 31, 40, 45, 46–47
Busby, John, 75, 76, 146*n*
Butter, Nathaniel, 33–35, 75, 128, 135

Campbell, Hay, 152*n*
Capell, Edward, 69
Carroll, D. Allen, 44, 141*n*
Cartwright, William, 62
*Catalogue of such English Bookes, as lately haue
  bene, and now are in Printing for
  Publication* (W. Jaggard), 61
Catherine and Petruchio (Garrick), 91
Cervantes, Miguel de, 62
Chamberlain's men, 54
Chambers, E. K., 44, 141*n*, 143*n*, 146*n*,
  149*n*
Changeling, The (Middleton and Rowley), 90
Charles I, King of England, 93
Chartier, Roger, 5, 137*n*, 156*n*

Chettle, Henry, 45
Chetwind, Philip, 64
Chetwood, William Rufus, 149*n*
Christian Turn'd Turke, A (Daborne), 139*n*
Cibber, Colley, 95, 154*n*
Clarke, Mary Cowden, 97
Clarke, Sampson, 35
Clarke, W. G., 82, 147*n*
Cobbler's Prophecy, The (Wilson), 47
Cockpit playhouse, 20, 89
collaboration:
  authorial, 17, 64–72
  in printing house, 16, 67, 69, 72, 77, 78,
    118, 121, 123
  in theater, 14–15, 16, 17, 20, 26, 48, 68,
    69, 71, 72, 74, 77, 78, 88, 119, 134, 136
Collier, Jeremy, 84
Colman, George, 86, 149*n*
Columbia University, 128
Common Wealth of England (Smith), 48
Condell, Henry, 9, 15, 20, 50, 52, 53, 79, 98
  as Shakespeare folio (1623) editor, 54–55,
    57–60, 71–78
Connor, Patrick W., 127, 157*n*
copyright, 23–24, 25, 52, 96, 134, 150*n*
Corballis, Richard, 152*n*
Coriolanus (Shakespeare), 95
Cotes, Richard, 79
Cotes, Thomas, 79–80
Courthope, W. J., 141*n*
Covell, William, 150*n*
Creede, Thomas, 47, 140*n*
Cymbeline (Shakespeare), 61
Cynthia's Revenge (Jonson), 140*n*

Daborne, Robert, 139*n*
Daniel, Samuel, 25, 26, 47, 140*n*
Danter, John, 22, 44–48
Davenant, William, 89–90, 95, 145*n*
Davenport, Robert, 16
Dávidházi, Péter, 150*n*
Davies, John, 143*n*
Dawson, Anthony, 138*n*
Dawson, Giles E., 147*n*, 151*n*
Declaration of Egregious Popish Impostures
  (Harsnett), 30
de Grazia, Margreta, 103, 145*n*, 146*n*,
  152*n*–53*n*, 154*n*
Dekker, Thomas, 45
Dennis, John, 95
Derby's men, 40
Dering, Edward, 61, 72, 146*n*

Dessen, Alan C., 138*n*
Devil Is an Ass, The (Jonson), 144*n*
Devil's Charter, The (Barnes), 19–20
Dewe, Thomas, 35–40
Digges, Leonard, 54
Dobson, Michael, 97, 151*n*
Donaldson, Peter S., 128, 157*n*
Donaldson v. Beckett, 150*n*
Don Quixote (Cervantes), 62
Double Falsehood (Theobald), 93–95, 94,
    149*n*
Downes, John, 86, 89, 90, 145*n*, 148*n*,
    149*n*
Drake, James, 84
Drayton, Michael, 30, 48,
Dr. Faustus (Marlowe), 21
Droeshout, Martin, 69
Drummond, William, 64
Drury Lane playhouse, 95
Dryden, John, 85, 86, 88, 97, 148*n*, 149*n*,
    150*n*
Duchess of Malfi, The (Webster), 7–8, 17–19
Duguid, Paul, 155*n*
Duke's men, 90
Duncan-Jones, Katherine, 138*n*
Dunciad, The (Pope), 91
Dutton, Richard, 147*n*

Eagleton, Terry, 9, 139*n*
E. and J. Wright, 107–9
e-books, 114
Eco, Umberto, 158*n*
editorial theory, 24–25, 117–23, 125–29
    authorial intentions in, 3–4, 16, 118–19,
        120–23, 127, 129
    biblical criticism and, 97, 109–10
    in eighteenth century, 95–110
    electronic texts and, 125–27, 128–29
    "ideal text" in, 3–4, 16, 117, 119–20, 122,
        125, 127
    platonic tradition of, 117–19, 122, 156*n*
    Pope's contribution to, 99–100
    pragmatic tradition of, 117–18
Egerton, Stephen, 25–26, 47, 140*n*
Eggert, Paul, 157*n*
Eisenstein, Elizabeth L., 112, 155*n*
electronic texts, 111–17, 125–33
    authorial intentions in, 113, 127, 129, 135
    capaciousness of, 125, 127–29, 130,
        132–33, 136
    critical editions as, 119, 125
    editorial theory and, 125–27, 128–29

as fluid and permeable, 144–15, 116, 125,
    127, 130, 132, 133, 136
of *Hamlet*, 128–29
of *King Lear*, 126, 128–29
physical disadvantages of, 113–14
possible demise of printed books caused
    by, 1, 2, 5, 111, 112, 113, 131, 155*n*
readers and, 113, 127, 155*n*
"real presence" of, 112–13, 135
technology of, 111–15, 125, 130–32
English Civil War, 83, 93
English Stock, 63
Essay of Dramatick Poetry (Dryden), 148*n*
Essays (Montaigne), 62
Evelyn, John, 85, 148*n*
Every Man Out Of His Humor (Jonson), 17, 18

Fairie Queene (Spenser), 62
Family of Love, The (Middleton), 31
Family Shakespeare (Bowdler and Bowdler),
    109–10
Farmer, Alan, 140*n*, 156*n*
Feinnes, Joseph, 121
Ferguson, W. Craig, 142*n*
Field, Richard, 6
Fielding, Henry, 102
Fitzgeffrey, Henry, 63, 144*n*
Fletcher, John, 21, 67–68, 69, 83, 84, 88,
    146*n*–47*n*, 148*n*
Fletcher, Robert, 50
Florio, John, 62
Flower, Francis, 45
Four Prentices of London, The (Heywood),
    139*n*
Foxon, David, 152*n*
Frankfurt book fair, 60, 61
Franklin, Colin, 149*n*, 153*n*
Freehafer, John, 149*n*
Frick Museum, 11

Garrick, David, 91, 107, 153*n*–54*n*
Geduld, Harry M., 151*n*, 152*n*
Genest, J. P., 96, 150*n*
Genette, Gerard, 155*n*
Globe theater, 8, 89, 141*n*
Glover, John, 82, 147*n*
Goldman, Michael, 6, 138*n*
Gollancz, Isaac, 143*n*
Gonderis, Joanna, 153
Gosson, Henry, 66
Gouge, William, 139*n*
Graham, Walter, 149*n*

Greene, Robert, 48
Greene's Tu quoque (Cooke), 33
Greetham, D. C., 156n
Greg, W. W., 44, 53, 73, 76, 102, 118,
    141n–42n, 143n, 153n, 157n
Griffiths, Ralph, 107, 154n
Grundy, Isobel, 153n

Halliday, F. E., 152n
Hamlet (Shakespeare), 9, 11, *12*, 26–30, *28*,
    48, 73, 75, 81, 85, 123, 128–29, 133,
    134, 136
Hamlet, The (Faulkner), 134
Hammond, Brean S., 149n
Hanmer, Thomas, 103, 152n
Hapgood, Robert, 138n
Harsnett, Samuel, 30
Hart, John A., 152n
Hawkins, Richard, 31, 79, 80, 147n
Hayes, Thomas, 29
Helme, John, 35–40
Heminge, John, 9, 15, 20, 50, 52, 53, 79, 98
    as Shakespeare folio (1623) editor, 54–55,
    57–60, 67–69, 71–78
Henningman, Henry, 98
Henry IV Part One (Shakespeare), 10, 21, 31,
    33, 81, 85, 105
Henry V (Shakespeare), 17, *19*, *59*, 75–76, 79,
    95, 120–21
Henry VI Part One (Shakespeare), 31
Henry VI Part Two (Shakespeare), 31, 75, 79,
    95
Henry VI Part Three (Shakespeare), 75, 79
Henry VIII (Shakespeare), 67, 68, 85, 99,
    145n
Herbert, Philip, 50, 71–72
Herbert, William, 50, 71–72
Hero and Leander (Marlowe), 62, 63, 144n
Herringham, Henry, 148n
Heylyn, Peter, 83–84, 148n
Heywood, Thomas, 20, 24, 33, 52, 53–54,
    55–57, 139n, 140n, 142n–43n, 150n
Hibbard, G. R., 129
Hickson, Samuel, 145n
Hill, Aaron, 95
Hodgdon, Barbara, 138n
Holinshed, Raphael, 128
Holland, Peter, 151n, 157n
Honest Whore, The (Dekker), 45
Honigmann, E. A. J., 155n
Hope, Jonathan, 145n
Hoppe, Harry, 142n

Howard-Hill, Trevor, 144n–45n
Hudson, H. N., 88, 149n
Hugo, Victor, 132
Hulme, T. E., 116, 156n
Hume, David, 149n
Hume, Robert D., 149n, 150n
Hunchback of Notre Dame, The (Hugo), 132
Hunsdon's men, 54

"ideal text," 3–4, 16, 117, 119–20, 122, 125,
    127
internet, 111, 113, *126*, 127, 128–29, 131
Ioppolo, Grace, 145n, 153n

Jackson, Alfred, 151n
Jackson, MacDonald P., 145n
Jackson, William A., 143n, 144n
Jaggard, Dorothy, 79
Jaggard, Isaac, 79, 143n–44n, 147n
    as printer and publisher of Shakespeare
    folio (1623), 55, 60, 61
Jaggard, William, 40, 55–61, 78, 80, 128,
    135
    Pavier quartos printed by, 55, 57, 65
    in printing of Shakespeare folio (1623),
    55, 57–61, 65, 66, 68
Jarvis, Simon, 97, 151n, 152n
Jenkins, Harold, 129
Jesus Psalter, 45
Johns, Adrian, 155n
Johnson, Arthur, 76, 80, 146n, 147n
Johnson, Gerald D., 29, 140n–41n, 145n
Johnson, Samuel, 8, 9, 53, 86, 100, 101,
    102, 103, 107, *108*, 138n, 142n, 147n,
    148n, 152n, 153n, 154n
Jones, R. F., 152n
Jonson, Ben, 9, 55, 65, 83, 84, 148n, 150n
    literary authority claimed by, 17, 52, 53,
    63, 66, 71, 77, 78
Jonson folios, 53, 55, 63–64, 72, 84, 144n
Jowett, John, 145n
Joyce, Michael, 115, 156n
Judge, Cyril Bathurst, 140n
Julius Caesar (Shakespeare), 85, 99, 153n

Keats, John, 109, 154n
Killigrew, Thomas, 90
King John and Matilda (Davenport), 16
King John (Shakespeare), 95, 99, 123
King Lear (Shakespeare), 33–35, *34*, 75, 81,
    83, 86–88, *87*, 91, 109, 123, *126*, 128,
    130, 135

King's men, 8, 14–15, 19, 35, 48, 57, 65, 68, 74, 83, 141*n*
King's men (Killigrew's), 90
Kirkman, Francis, 97, 150*n*
Kirschbaum, Leo, 143*n*
Kiséry, András, 150*n*
Knight of the Burning Pestle, The (Beaumont), 33, 141*n*
Knowles, Richard, 157*n*
Konkola, Karin, 139*n*
Kyd, Thomas, 21

Landow, George P., 115, 125, 156*n*, 157*n*
Lanham, Richard, 155*n*
Latin, 45, 81
Lavagnino, John, 133, 158*n*
Law, Robert Adger, 145*n*
Lee, Nathaniel, 150*n*
Lee, Sidney, 143*n*
Lesser, Zachary, 141*n*
Levenson, E. A., 137*n*
Levinson, Jill L., 142*n*
libraries, 2, 22, 72, 128, 130, 139*n*, 146*n*
licensing of print, 23, 46
Lincoln's Inn playhouse, 95
Ling, Nicholas, 27–30, 44, 47, 48, 140*n*
London Gazette, 98
London Magazine, 153*n*–54*n*
London Prodigall, The (anon.), 35, 37
Lords, House of, 96, 150*n*
Love's Labor's Lost (Shakespeare), 31, 32, 47, 48, 55, 75, 81
Lowin, John, 90, 145*n*
Lucrece (Shakespeare), 6
Lyly, John, 62

Macbeth (Shakespeare), 68, 81–82, 95, 99, 145*n*
McGann, Jerome J., 117–18, 137*n*, 156*n*, 157
McKenzie, D. F., 3, 137*n*–38*n*, 144*n*, 156*n*
McKerrow, R. B., 44, 62, 73, 76, 118, 141*n*, 144*n*, 153*n*, 156*n*
McLeod, Randy, 156*n*
McMillin, Scott, 144*n*
Maguire, Laurie E., 24–25, 140*n*, 143*n*
Maguire, Nancy, 148*n*
Malcontent, The (Marston), 45
Malone, Edmond, 69, 76, 80, 103, 107–9, 146*n*, 147*n*, 154*n*
manuscript plays, 67, 68
    price paid by publishers for, 22, 23, 140*n*

as property of acting companies, 17, 47, 68
Shakespeare and, 10, 47, 69, 72–75, 82, 111, 121, 124, 136, 142*n*, 157*n*
types of, 25
Mantuan, 81
Marcus, Leah, 140*n*, 145*n*, 154*n*
Marder, Harry M., 154*n*
Marder, Louis, 151*n*
Mariot, Richard, 148*n*
Marlowe, Christopher, 14, 21, 55, 62
Marsden, Jean I., 91, 148*n*, 149*n*
Martyn, John, 148*n*
masques, 25
Masten, Jeffrey, 147*n*, 154*n*
Master of the Revels, 20, 64
Meighen, Richard, 79, 80, 144*n*, 147*n*
memorial reconstruction, 27–29, 46, 65, 73, 76
Merchant of Venice, The (Shakespeare), 29, 83
Meres, Francis, 150*n*
Merry Wives of Windsor, The (Shakespeare), 75–76, 80
Middleton, Thomas, 31, 68
Millington, Thomas, 75, 76
Milton, John, 127
Mincoff, Marco, 145*n*
Mist's Journal, 99
Mitchell, William J., 2 137*n*
Monarchick Tragedies, The (Alexander), 62
Montaigne, Michel de, 62
Montgomery, William, 145*n*
Morley, Henry, 151*n*
Moseley, Humphrey, 146*n*–47*n*
Mowat, Barbara A., 151*n*, 157*n*
Mucedorus (anon.), 21
Much Ado About Nothing (Shakespeare), 99
Murphy, Andrew, 142*n*, 158*n*
Murphy, Arthur, 97

New Bibliography, 44–45, 47, 73–74, 101, 157*n*
New Criticism, 3
Nicoll, Allardyce, 149*n*

Okes, Nicholas, 33
Oras, Ants, 145*n*
Orgel, Stephen, 8, 138*n*, 145*n*, 154*n*–55*n*, 157*n*, 158*n*
Orlando Furioso (Greene), 47
Osborne, Laurie E., 150*n*

Othello (Shakespeare), 9, 27, 35, 80, 81, 83, 85

Painful Adventures of Pericles, Prince of Tyre, The (Wilkins), 65
paper, 3, 5, 22, 50–51, 100, 107, 123
Paradise Lost (Milton), 127
Partridge, A. C., 145*n*
Partridge, Robert C. Barrington, 146*n*
Passionate Pilgrim, The, 55–57, *56*, *58*
Pavier, Thomas, 55, 57, *59*, 66, 75, 80, 128, 147*n*
Pembroke's men, 40, 54
Percy, Thomas, 107–9, 154*n*
performance, performed plays, 121, 129, 133
    advertised on play title pages, 7–8, 19, *19*, 31, *32*, 33, *34*, 35–40, *36*, *37*, *38*, *39*, *41*, *42*, *43*, 47–48, *59*, 71, *94*, 96
    Augustan adaptations of, 91–96, 100, 109
    authorial intentions in, 14–15, 86, 88, 91
    ephemerality of, 7, 8
    print compared with, 6–9
    Restoration adaptations of, 84–91, 124, 134
    Shakespeare's interest in, 5–7, 9, 10, 11, 64, 69, 71, 88, 111
    see also acting companies
Pericles (Shakespeare), 64–66, 89, 123
Philaster (Beaumont and Fletcher), 31
Philips, Ian, 146*n*
Phillips, Ambrose, 95
Pickering, John, 155*n*
piracy, 24–25, 27, 29, 30, 44, 46, 140*n*
playbills, 150*n*
playwrights, *see* authors, authorship
Plomer, Henry R., 45, 142*n*
Poems (Drayton), 48
poetry, Shakespeare's commitment to printing of, 6, 138*n*
Pollard, A. W., 73, 76, 83, 143*n*, 146*n*, 147*n*
Ponsonby, William, 61–62, 144*n*
Pope, Alexander, 91, 97, 99–101, 102, 119–20, 151*n*, 152*n*
Porson, Richard, 103–7
Practice of Piety, The (Bayley), 10
print, printed books, 1–13
    authorial intentions in, 3–4, 5, 17–20, 26, 73, 113, 116, 118–19, 120–23, 135–36
    fixity and self-containment of, 15, 114–15, 116, 124–25, 127, 129, 130, 132, 133–34, 135, 136, 139*n*

as force of repression, 112
history contained in, 5, 7, 9, 15–16, 17, 116, 122–23
meaning created by, 2–3, 4–5, 137*n*
as neutral containers of texts, 3, 4, 5, 117, 119
performance compared with, 6–9
physical comforts of, 113–14
predicted demise of, 1, 2, 5, 111, 112, 113, 131, 155*n*
"real presence" of, 112–13, 135, 155*n*
technology of, 1–2, 5, 115–16, 131–32
texts in, 4–5, 8–9, 26–30, 45–46, 95–110, 112, 116, 117–20, 124–25, 135
"work" compared with, 4, 117
printed plays:
    financial risk in printing of, 21–23, 76
    numbers of, 20–22, 23, 83
    print-runs of, 22–23
    publisher marketing of, 31–40
    publishing costs of, 22–23, 143*n*
    retail prices of, 23, 31, 72
    single-play folio editions of, 51
    subliterary status of, 17, 21, 22, 26, 31, 46, 48, 49, 72
    see also specific editions and plays
printing, shared, 45
prompt books, 69, 73
Prynne, William, 5, 221–22, 138*n*, 139*n*
"Publique Faith, The" (Fletcher), 50
publishers:
    definition of, 60
    financial risk assumed by, 143*n*
    marketing strategies of, 31–40
    opportunistic play publishing of, 22–23, 50
    piracy and, 24–25, 27, 29, 30, 44, 46, 140*n*
    profit as goal of, 22–23, 24, 25, 26, 30, 48–49, 75, 124, 135
    of Shakespeare folios, 40, 55–63, 65–66, 77–78, 79–80
    unauthorized publication and, 20, 23–24, 25–26, 27, 29, 33–35, 47, 52, 73, 74
    see also specific publishers

Queen's men, 35, 141*n*

Raleigh, Walter, 55
Rape of Lucrece (Heywood), 20
readers, 3, 4–5, 31, 49, 82–83, 130, 132, 135
    electronic texts and, 113, 127, 155*n*

of Shakespeare folio (1623), 20, 63, 71, 72, 77–78
Reed, Isaac, 103
reported texts, *see* memorial reconstruction
Rhodes, John, 89
Rhodes, R. Crompton, 61, 143*n*
Rich, John, 93–95
Richard II (Shakespeare), 10, 21, 31, 33, 91–92
Richard III (Shakespeare), 10, 21, 31, 33, 75
right to copy, 23–24, 27, 29, 40, 44, 45–46, 47, 75, 76, 140*n*, 146*n*
in publication of Shakespeare folios, 61, 64, 65, 66, 79–80
Roberts, Alexander, 140*n*
Roberts, John, 27–30
Robinson, Ben, 142*n*–43*n*
Rochester, Earl of, 88
RocketBook, 114
Rogers, Malcolm, 139*n*
Romeo and Juliet (Shakespeare), 31, 40–48, *41, 42, 43,* 73, 75, 86, 91, 98, 142*n*
Rose, Mark, 150*n*, 158*n*
Rowe, Nicholas, 96, 98–99, 100–101, 103, *105*, 124, 151*n*, 153*n*

Sacks, Richard, 128
Sams, Eric, 141*n*
Schollers Purgatory, The (Wither), 140*n*
scribal copies, 10, 25, 67, 69, 73
Seary, Peter, 152*n*
Second Part of the Return From Parnassus (anon.), 22
Sejanus (Jonson), 17, 66
sermons, 21–22, 25–26
Shaaber, Matthias, 80, 147*n*
Shakespeare, William:
authorial manuscripts of, 10, 47, 69, 72–75, 82, 111, 121, 124, 136, 142*n*, 157*n*
collaborative authorship and, 64–72
cultural prestige of, 10, 13, 14, 77, 82, 84, 97–98, 109
iconography of, 10, 14
performance as interest of, 5–7, 9, 10, 11, 64, 69, 71, 88, 111
as shareholder in King's men, 14–15, 16, 54, 67–68, 147*n*
single authorship and, 14–15, 16, 68–71, 77, 78, 111, 145*n*
stained-glass representation of, 10, 11

uninvolved in play publication, 5–7, 10–11, 15, 16, 20–21, 33–35, 48–49, 52–54, 74, 78, 111, 118, 135, 136
will of, 54
Shakespeare, William, works of:
Augustan adaptations of, 91–96, 100, 109
"bad quartos" of, 26–30, 44, 45–47, 72–76, 134
best-selling plays of, 10–11, 20–21, 22, 65
bibles printed on worse paper than, 5
Cambridge Globe edition of, 82, 124
facsimiles of, 107–9, 123, 128, 154*n*
film versions of, 14, 53, 121, 127, 128, 133
Johnson–Steevens edition of, 86, 101, 102, 103, 107, *108*
modernized editions of, 80–83, 84, 85, 91, 99–100, 123
number of editions of, 20–21, 22, 33, 65, 83
as "old-fashioned," 84–95, 90, 97
Oxford edition of, 65, 120–121, 124, 128
poems of, 6, 22, 138*n*
Pope's edition of, 91, 97, 99–101
Restoration adaptations of, 84–91, 124, 134
revisions of, 68, 142*n*
Rowe's edition of, 96, 98–99, 100–101, 103, *105*, 124, 151*n*, 152*n*, 153*n*
Shakespeare named on title pages of, *28,* 30–31, *32,* 33–44, *34, 37, 39, 43,* 47–49, 55–57, *56,* 64, 71, 93, *94,* 134
Shakespeare uninvolved in publication of, 5–7, 10–11, 15, 16, 20–21, 33–35, 48–49, 52–54, 74, 78, 111, 118, 135, 136
in Suckling portrait, 11–13, *12*
Theobald's edition of, 97, 98, 100–103, 152*n*–53*n*
variorum editions of, 103–7, *106*
see also specific editions and plays
"Shakespeare Electronic Archive, The," 128–29
Shakespeare folio (1623), 8, 21, 40, 49, 50–78, 79–83, 99, 101, 128, 135, 153*n*
bookseller advertisments for, 60, 61
collaborative plays omitted from, 64–67, 68–69
commendatory verses in, 9, 52, 54, 69, 71
engraved portrait in, 52, 69, *70*
Heminge and Condell dedication in, 9, 15, 20, 50, 52, 55, 71–78, 98
physical size of, 50–52

Shakespeare folio (1623) (*cont.*)
  players named in, 71
  publishing syndicate of, 40, 55–63,
    65–66, 77–78, 79
  quality of texts in, 72–77, 80–83
  readers of, 20, 63, 71, 72, 77–78
  retail price of, 72
  rights to plays in, 61, 64, 65, 66
  risk in publishing of, 57–60, 61, 63,
    77–78
  Shakespeare uninvolved in, 52–53, 78
  title page of, 64, 69, *70*, 71
Shakespeare folio (1632), 63, 79–83, 101
  changes from first folio in, 80–83
  publishing syndicate of, 79–80
  rights to plays in, 79–80
Shakespeare folio (1664), 64, 83, 84, 85
Shakespeare folio (1685), 84, 85, 98
Shakespeare in Love, 14, 53, 121
Shelton, Thomas, 62
Sherbo, Arthur, 152*n*
Shillingsburg, Peter L., 156*n*
Sidney, Philip, 62
Siege of Rhodes (Davenant), 90
Silberman, Steve, 155*n*–56*n*
Simone, Raffaele, 135, 158*n*
Sir John Oldcastle Part One (anon.), 57
Sir Thomas More, 64, 66, 121, 136
Sixe Court Comedies (Lyly), 62
Smethwick, John, 29, 40–44, 47–48, 60, 61,
    78, 79, 80, 147*n*
Smith, Thomas, 48
Sorelius, Gunner, 148*n*
Spanish Tragedy (Kyd), 21
Spedding, James, 68, 145*n*
Spencer, Hazelton, 148*n*
Spenser, Edmund, 62
Stafford, Simon, 66
Stallybrass, Peter, 154*n*
Staple of News, The (Jonson), 144*n*
Stationers' Company, 11, 23–24, 45, 46, 47,
    48, 57, 66, 72, 75, 80
Steevens, George, 80, 86, 103, 107, *108*,
    147*n*, 148*n*–49*n*, 154*n*
Steiner, George, 112–13, 155*n*
Stephens, John, 140*n*
Stoddard, Roger, 115–16, 156*n*
Stone, George Winchester, 154
Suckling, John, 11–13, *12*, 51
Sussex's men, 40
Swinburne, Algernon Charles, 57, 143*n*
Swinhowe, George, 63

Taming of A Shrew, The (Shakespeare), 20, 48
Taming of the Shrew, The (Shakespeare), 31
Tanselle, G. Thomas, 117–18, 122, 137*n*,
    156*n*, 157*n*
Tate, Nahum, 86–88, *87*, 91, 154*n*
Taylor, Gary, 65, 120–21, 138*n*, 143*n*, 145*n*,
    151*n*, 154*n*, 158*n*
Taylor, Neil, 129
Tempest, The (Shakespeare), 99
textual criticism, *see* editorial theory
theater companies, *see* acting companies
Theatres Royal, 96
Theobald, Lewis, 91–95, 96–97, 98,
    100–103, 149*n*, 151*n*, 152*n*, 153*n*
  Pope critiqued by, 91
  Richard II adaptation of, 91–95
Thompson, Ann, 129
Thorpe, Thomas, 138*n*
Tilney, Edward, 64
Timon of Athens (Shakespeare), 99
title pages, 26, 27–29
  authors named on, 17, *18*, 19–20, *28*,
    30–31, *32*, 33–44, *34*, *37*, *39*, *43*, 47–49,
    55–57, *56*, 64, 71, 93, *94*, 134
  performance attributions on, 7–8, 17, 19,
    19, 31, *32*, 33, *34*, 35–40, *36*, *37*, *38*, *39*,
    41, *42*, *43*, 47–48, *59*, 71, *94*, 96
  of Shakespeare folio (1623), 64, 69, *70*, 71
  variant, 40–44, 57, 141*n*
Titus Andronicus (Shakespeare), 31, 40, 44,
    46, 79, 81
Tonson, Jacob, 98, 99, 100–101, 151*n*, 152*n*
Tonson family, 152*n*–53*n*
Townesend, Philip, 144*n*
Treatise of Moral Philosophy (Baldwin), 10
Troilus and Cressida (Shakespeare), 8, 23, 33,
    64, 85, 91, 141*n*
Troublesome Raigne of King John, The (anon.),
    35–40, *38*, *39*, 141*n*
True Chronicle History of King Leir, The
    (anon.), 35, *36*
Trundle, John, 27–30
Two Noble Kinsmen, The (Shakespeare and
    Fletcher), 64, 66
type, typefaces, 3, 5, 22, 31, 45

Updike, John, 113
"Upon *Aglaura* Printed in Folio" (Brome),
    51

Van Dyck, Anthony, 11–13, *12*
Venus and Adonis (Shakespeare), 6, 22

Vickers, Brian, 30, 86, 141*n*, 148*n*–49*n*, 151*n*, 154*n*
Vickers, Samuel, 144*n*
Virginia company, 54
Vision of the Twelve Goddesses (Daniel), 25

W., J., 143*n*
Walkley, Thomas, 35, 40, 80, 147*n*
Waller, Edmund, 88
Walsh, Marcus, 97, 151*n*
Warburton, William, 102, 103, *104*, 149*n*, 153*n*
Ward, John, 83–84, 148*n*
Warren, Austin, 3, 137*n*
Warton, Joseph, 89
Webster, John, 7–8, 17–19, 150*n*
Weimann, Robert, 8, 138*n*
Wellek, René, 3, 137*n*
Wells, Stanley, 6, 65, 120, 138*n*, 145*n*, 157*n*
Werstine, Paul, 146*n*, 153*n*
White, Edward, 44

Whole-Armor of God, The (Gouge), 139*n*
Wild-Goose Chase, The (Fletcher), 84
Wilkins, George, 65
Williams, George Walton, 141*n*
Williams, W. P., 144*n*
Wilson, J. Dover, 118, 156*n*
Windet, John 24
Winter's Tale, The (Shakespeare), 81, 154*n*
Wise, Andrew, 75
Wither, George, 23–24, 140*n*
Wittgenstein, Ludwig, 129, 158*n*
Wordsworth, William, 4
Workes (Dering), 61
Works (Beaumont and Fletcher), 88
Works (Shakespeare), 95–110, *104*, *105*, *106*, *108*, 152*n*–53*n*
Worthen, W. B., 138*n*
Wynne, Richard and Owen, 143*n*

Yorkshire Tragedy (anon.), 57